PENGUIN BOOKS

# THE PASSION

Geza Vermes was born in Hungary in 1924. He studied in Budapest and Louvain, where he read Oriental history and languages and in 1953 obtained a doctorate in theology with a dissertation on the Dead Sea Scrolls. From 1957 to 1991 he taught at the Universities of Newcastle and Oxford. His pioneering work on the Dead Sea Scrolls and the historical figure of Jesus led to his appointment as the first Professor of Jewish Studies at Oxford, where he is now Professor Emeritus. Since 1991 he has been director of the Forum for Qumran Research at the Oxford Centre for Hebrew and Jewish Studies. Professor Vermes is a Fellow of the British Academy and of the European Academy of Arts, Sciences and Humanities, the holder of an Oxford D.Litt. and of honorary doctorates from several British universities. Professor Vermes's books include *The Complete Dead Sea Scrolls in English* (1997), *The Changing Faces of Jesus* (2000) and *The Authentic Gospel of Jesus* (2003), all published by Penguin.

# GEZA VERMES

# *The Passion*

PENGUIN BOOKS

PENGUIN BOOKS

Published by the Penguin Group
Penguin Group (USA) Inc., 375 Hudson Street, New York, New York 10014, U.S.A.
Penguin Group (Canada), 90 Eglinton Avenue East, Suite 700, Toronto,
Ontario, Canada M4P 2Y3 (a division of Pearson Penguin Canada Inc.)
Penguin Books Ltd, 80 Strand, London WC2R 0RL, England
Penguin Ireland, 25 St Stephen's Green, Dublin 2, Ireland (a division of Penguin Books Ltd)
Penguin Group (Australia), 250 Camberwell Road, Camberwell,
Victoria 3124, Australia (a division of Pearson Australia Group Pty Ltd)
Penguin Books India Pvt Ltd, 11 Community Centre, Panchsheel Park, New Delhi – 110 017, India
Penguin Group (NZ), cnr Airborne and Rosedale Roads, Albany,
Auckland 1310, New Zealand (a division of Pearson New Zealand Ltd)
Penguin Books (South Africa) (Pty) Ltd, 24 Sturdee Avenue,
Rosebank, Johannesburg 2196, South Africa

Penguin Books Ltd, Registered Offices:
80 Strand, London WC2R 0RL, England

First published by Penguin Books (UK) 2005
First published in the United States of America by Penguin Books (USA) 2006

1 3 5 7 9 8 6 4 2

ISBN 0 14 30.3688 2

Printed in the United States of America

# Contents

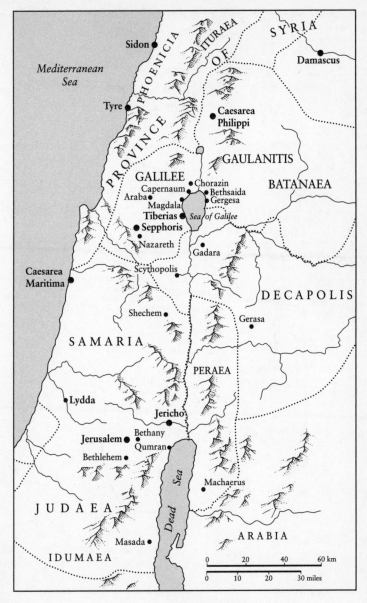

*Palestine in the age of Jesus*

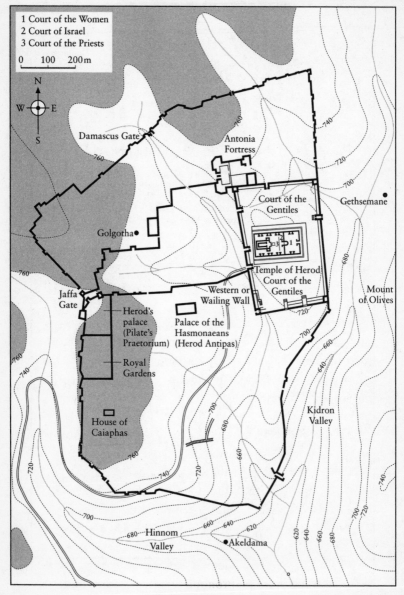

1 Court of the Women
2 Court of Israel
3 Court of the Priests

0   100   200m

N
W     E
S

Damascus Gate

Antonia
Fortress

Court of the
Gentiles

Gethsemane

Golgotha

Temple of Herod
Court of the
Gentiles

Mount
of Olives

Jaffa
Gate

Western or
Wailing Wall

Herod's
palace
(Pilate's
Praetorium)

Palace of the
Hasmonaeans
(Herod Antipas)

Royal
Gardens

Kidron
Valley

House of
Caiaphas

Hinnom
Valley

Akeldama

*The Jerusalem of Jesus*

# *Preface*

The traditional version of the Passion of Jesus is coherent and straightforward, even simple. Whether it is preached from the pulpit or read in literature of piety, the story hardly varies. It may even be watched in the cinema: *The Passion of the Christ* by Mel Gibson, the international box-office hit of 2004, is still fresh in many people's minds. This is a story which is meant to be perceived with the eyes of faith. It recounts the sacrifice, the self-immolation of the Son of God who willingly offered his life, we are told, for the redemption of the sins of mankind. Without exception all the children of Adam have to accept their own responsibility for it if they are to reap the fruits of the atonement achieved for them all by Christ dying on the cross.

But the same story has also an historical (or I would say pseudo-historical) dimension. It emanates from a simplistic and selective reading of the Gospels without appropriate interpretation, indeed without any interpretation. According to this version the suffering and death of Jesus were the outcome of the hostility and hatred of his enemies, the Jewish priestly leaders and their council, who browbeat the weak but basically decent Roman governor, Pontius Pilate, forcing him to pronounce Jesus guilty, and successfully harangued the multitude of their compatriots to clamour for his crucifixion. Here the responsibility for *deicide*, the murder of the divine Christ, is placed squarely on the shoulders of the Jewish people.

This representation of the Passion, which will be shown to be biased and twisted, has influenced the Christian world over most of its history. Even today, when the official spokesmen of churches, chapels and denominations reject what the great French historian Jules Isaac once called the doctrine of contempt, *l'enseignement du mépris*, many Christians, clergy and laity, have instinctively applauded the Passion *à la* Mel Gibson. Even the Pope is reported to have approved the version of the movie seen by him with the Delphic words, 'It is as it was.'

It goes without saying that, like everything else we know about Jesus, the account of his last day derives from the New Testament, and more specifically from the discrete narratives of the four Gospels. Unlike the traditional story produced by the Church, they are neither simple nor coherent. On the contrary, as we shall see, they are filled with discrepancies. Without a deliberate and artificial harmonization, which was already attempted in the centuries when Christendom was young and has continued ever since, they seem disconcerting and confusing. They form a mystery within which real history lurks.

To penetrate this mystery, the reader must come to grips with the literary sources that are closest to the reality of the Passion and subject Mark, Matthew, Luke and John, our four principal witnesses, to a stringent critical scrutiny. I like to compare the historian-interpreter to a detective charged with preparing a report to a law court. Four documents lie on his desk. He must pore over them, seek to clarify obscurities, establish facts and point out contradictions. In reality, the process will be simpler than it first appears since three out of the four narratives of the Passion closely resemble one another. Two of them, Mark and Matthew, are nearly identical. In consequence, they can be surveyed together, grasped in a single glance, *synoptically*, while separate treatment is reserved for the occasional, but often momentous, divergences between the narratives, especially in the Gospel of Luke. Finally, the comparison of Mark, Matthew and Luke – the Synoptics – with the Fourth Gospel will make plain that the events of the last day of the life of Jesus have been transmitted in two fundamentally different traditions. To define, evaluate and interpret these differences with the help of expert knowledge peppered with common sense is the momentous task facing this inquiry.

# Prologue

No attentive reader of the Gospels can fail to notice the striking contrast between the way the evangelists depict Jewish attitudes towards Jesus before the Passion and during the last few hours of his life.

Up until the fateful week in Jerusalem which ended with the crucifixion, Jesus appears as a charismatic healer and exorcist and a magnetic preacher, a greatly loved and much sought-after figure in the Galilean countryside around the Lake of Gennesaret. He attracted crowds. They avidly listened to him wherever he went, in synagogues, streets, public squares, on hillsides and on the lake shore. The rumour of his approach brought out the sick in droves. Those who were too weak to walk were carried to him on stretchers. Petty-minded synagogue presidents and quibbling village scribes envied him, and were overheard muttering words of disapproval. In their pedestrian thinking the blind, the lame and the lepers should have been cured, and the possessed delivered, on weekdays, not on the Sabbath. Insufficiently versed in Jewish theology, some Galilean scribes murmured 'blasphemy' when Jesus proclaimed that healing was the equivalent of forgiveness of sins, but even if they had dared to speak up, they would have been fighting a losing battle: the holy man from Nazareth enjoyed the trust and support of large segments of the local rural population. Both he and the crowd were familiar with the frame of mind of officialdom towards prophets of God. It did not bother them.

Not only in Galilee, but even on his arrival in Jerusalem, Jesus is portrayed as the hero of a joyful and welcoming crowd. He came to the holy city, according to the custom recorded by the Jewish historian Josephus, about a week before the feast (*Jewish War* 6:290). Mark, Matthew and John describe Jesus' approach to the capital as a triumphal entry universally acclaimed. Luke is less grandiose and ascribes the mood of festivity more specifically to the group of disciples who were the companions of Jesus. When observed more closely, the episode loses some of its intended radiance. Riding on a donkey was not that uncommon in the circumstances. We learn from rabbinic literature that ass drivers did lucrative business at the approach of festivals by hiring out their beasts to wealthy or important pilgrims. But the evangelists transform the incident into a royal messianic event, hailing the arrival of the Son of David. To make the messianic aspect more patent, Matthew cites the words of Zechariah, 'Behold your king is coming to you, humble and mounted on an ass, and on a colt, the foal of an ass.' 'On an ass' and 'on a colt, the foal of an ass' is of course the usual Hebrew poetic device of parallelism, the same idea being expressed in two similar expressions identical in meaning: they designate a single donkey. But in his zeal to equate prophecy and fulfilment, Matthew, unlike the other three evangelists, presents Jesus with two animals, a she-ass and her colt, and gives the impression that he was riding on both. The disciples put their garments 'on them', and Jesus sat 'on them'. To suggest that the first 'on them' refers to the animals and the second to the garments, smacks of special pleading. In fact, John corrects the misrepresentation by quoting, 'Behold your king is coming, sitting on an ass's colt.'

The Gospel account of Jesus' first two or three days in Jerusalem further attests indirectly that large groups were listening to his teaching in the Temple and that his patent popularity is given as the cause of why the priestly authorities abstained from immediately taking steps against him. In short, until his arrest Jesus seems to have been the darling of the Galilean country folk and even warmly welcomed by the Jewish crowd in Jerusalem.

Yet, if we are to believe the same evangelists, on the last day of the life of Jesus a sea-change suddenly occurred. Jesus became the object of hatred not only for the leaders of Judaism, the chief priests and the Sanhedrin, but also for the Jewish people at large. No one had a good word to say in his favour. Many witnesses testified against him, but none for him. The crowd abominated him. All the people, 'the Jews', asked for his death and egged on the Roman governor to crucify him. Luke, it is true, attempts to diminish the contrast by reporting that the previously hostile crowd present at the crucifixion beat their breasts after the death of Jesus, but this mitigating circumstance seems to be of the evangelist's own making, unsupported by Mark, Matthew or John.

What compelled the evangelists to present such an extraordinary contrast of pictures? How do the four Gospel accounts relate to one another and how do they tally with first-century AD Jewish and Roman reality as we know it from non-New Testament sources? What were the motives that influenced their chronicle of the Passion? These are the issues that the historian-exegete, or if you like the detective of the past, will have to investigate. He will assemble the evidence and inspect it through a magnifying glass before attempting to answer the final £1,000,000 question: What really happened on the day of the crucifixion of Jesus nearly 2,000 years ago?

# I

## Literary and historical preliminaries

### A. The sources

The Passion of Jesus of Nazareth is part of history, but it is also the central core of Christian theology, the very nucleus of the Church's faith. The four evangelists who convey their doctrinal message in the form of a biography of Jesus are not detached story-tellers; they do not intend to record the final hours of the life and the death of their hero in an objective manner or, to use Tacitus' famous phrase, *sine ira et studio*, without fear or favour. They have a religious message to preach in a form adapted to the needs of their specific readership. So before we set out to examine what the evangelists want us to *believe* about the Passion, we must ask who they were, whom they addressed and what motivated their writings.

According to mainstream scholarship these four authors produced their works between *c.* AD 70 and 110. None of them identifies himself explicitly in his Gospel, but early Christian tradition yields some information about each of them. Mark is thought to be the earliest. The other two, Matthew and Luke, largely depend on the Gospel of Mark in the general gist of their narrative and often even display verbal similarities in their Greek text. If any of the Gospels ever existed in a written Aramaic (or Hebrew) version, no trace of it has come down to us in manuscript form.

Mark is usually identified with John Mark, a cousin of Barnabas, the colleague of St Paul. He later became a companion of Paul himself, but is also alluded to by the pseudonymous author of the First Letter of Peter (*c.* AD 100) as Peter's close associate. Outside the New Testament the earliest reference to Mark comes from a now lost work of Papias, an early second-century AD writer, quoted by the fourth-century Church historian Eusebius of Caesarea (*c.* 260–340). If Papias is to be believed, Mark was Peter's assistant, and wrote his Gospel at the instigation of the Roman Christians. Papias also states that Mark was not a direct witness of the Gospel events, but recorded the preaching of Peter. Christian tradition credits Mark with the establishment of the Church in Egypt. The large majority of modern scholars date Mark's account of the life and teaching of Jesus to the time of the first war between the Jews and the Romans (AD 66–74), more likely to the years following the destruction of Jerusalem in AD 70, that is, some forty years or so after the Passion.

Matthew is also mentioned by Papias. He is introduced as the compiler of the Sayings of Jesus written in the Hebrew dialect, i.e. in Aramaic, the common language of Palestinian Jews. Since no excerpts of these have been preserved, no one knows whether the Sayings are identical with the actual Gospel of Matthew or are only parts of it, and whether this Matthew is one of the twelve apostles of Jesus. Matthew's biblical quotations, which often make sense only on the basis of the Greek Old Testament, suggest that he was probably a Greek-speaking Jew. Most contemporary New Testament scholars place Matthew's work to *c.* AD 80–100.

Luke, the non-Jewish author of the Third Gospel, is believed to have been one of Paul's close associates. The earliest representation of Luke as an evangelist and the author of the Acts of the Apostles comes from the Muratorian Canon, the most ancient catalogue of the books of the New Testament, contained in an eighth-century Milanese manuscript and published in 1740 by L. A. Muratori. The original document is thought to date to *c.* AD 180.

The identity of the evangelist John is unascertainable. Apart from the title, 'according to John', the Gospel itself from chapter 1 to chapter 20 mentions no author. In chapter 21, someone distinct from the evangelist attempts to make him out to be 'the beloved disciple of Jesus'. This hint *tacitly* assumes that the Galilean fisherman John, the son of Zebedee and an eyewitness of the ministry of Jesus, was the fourth evangelist.

Now, the Church father Irenaeus, bishop of Lyons, reported *c.* AD 180 that the apostle John lived to a great age in the city of Ephesus in western Asia Minor, and produced the Fourth Gospel there. However, no New Testament evidence confirms this statement to connect John with Ephesus. The martyr bishop Ignatius of Antioch had a splendid opportunity to testify to John's presence in Ephesus, but failed to do so. In his letter to the members of the church of that city, written *c.* AD 110, he referred to the Ephesians as the people of Paul, and not as the children of John, who had lived among them only a few years earlier.

To envisage the author of the Fourth Gospel as an 'uneducated and common' Galilean fisherman (Acts 4:13), who was a centenarian, give or take a few years, yet was not only still creative but fully at home in Hellenistic mystical speculation, requires a leap of imagination which seems to be beyond the reasonable. In sum, the identity of the writer of the Fourth Gospel cannot be pinned down.

Regarding the date of this Gospel, the oldest known manuscript fragments of John belong to sometime between AD 125 and 150, and equally the oldest references to John's Gospel in early Christian literature come from the same period. So the work was completed before the mid-second century. On the other hand, the highly evolved doctrine of John demands that its composition should be placed after the redaction of the Synoptic Gospels, that is, after the last quarter of the first century AD. Likewise, the split reflected in John between Judaism and Christianity, with followers of Jesus being expelled from the synagogue, is hardly conceivable before the turn of the first century AD. The combined evidence suggests that the Fourth Gospel was published in the early second century, probably between the years AD 100 and 110. So the author of the Fourth Gospel is unlikely to have been a contemporary of the historical Jesus. None of the four authors seems to have been an eyewitness of the events chronicled in the Gospels. They completed their books forty to seventy years after the death of Jesus and relied on and transmitted traditions which they had inherited from various churches. The value of their testimony about the Passion will depend on the nature of the tradition transmitted by them.

The evangelists addressed their Gospels to those of their contemporaries whom they tried to persuade to embrace Christianity or to people who were already members of their churches. In other words, they either preached to convert or to the converted. Judging from their efforts to play down the Jewishness of Jesus, and the general anti-Jewish bent of the Passion stories, it is reasonable to deduce that the evangelization was no longer aimed at

Jews, but at the Gentile inhabitants of the Greek-speaking world. Indeed, the Jews are overwhelmingly depicted as the enemies of Jesus and his followers.

As far as the motivation is concerned, the story-tellers aim at presenting a Jewish Redeemer-Messiah crucified by Pontius Pilate so that he appears acceptable to the non-Jewish inhabitants of the Graeco-Roman world. The purpose of the evangelists is to prove implicitly that being a Christian is not incompatible with loyalty to Caesar and the Roman empire. Hence, as will be shown, they whitewash Pilate and Rome, and correspondingly deni-grate the Jewish leaders and through them the Jewish people at large.

## B. Jewish history and legal systems in force in Judaea in the age of Jesus

*The historical background*

The death of Jesus of Nazareth on the cross is an estab-lished fact, arguably the only established fact about him. It is attested not only by the four Gospels, the Acts of the Apostles and St Paul, but also outside the New Testament by Josephus ('Pilate ... condemned him to be crucified', *Jewish Antiquities* 18:64), Tacitus ('Christ ... had undergone the death penalty in the reign of Tiberius, by sentence of the procurator Pontius Pilate', *Annals* 15:44, 3) and, indirectly, by the Talmud ('On the eve of Passover they hanged Yeshu', Babylonian Talmud Sanhedrin 43a). The crucifixion is part of Jewish and Roman history of the first century AD. Therefore the historian must not treat it as an occurrence unique and *sui generis*, and any study of the Gospel accounts should be preceded by a survey of the chronological, cultural, religious and legal background of the Passion.

The life of Jesus began possibly in 6/5 BC, in the closing years of the reign of Herod the Great (37–4 BC), and ended during the governorship of Pontius Pilate (AD 26–36), probably in AD 30. His early childhood coincided with quarrels about the succession of Herod. Constant political turmoil was caused by a series of uprisings. The emperor Augustus divided the realm into three parts among the surviving sons of Herod. Archelaus was put in charge of Judaea, Idumaea and Samaria (4 BC–AD 6), Antipas of Galilee (4 BC–AD 39) and Philip of territories to the north and east of Galilee (4 BC–AD 33/34). None of them inherited the royal title.

Archelaus was dismissed by Augustus in AD 6. Judaea was then turned into a Roman province and the government of the country was transferred to a prefect, appointed by the emperor. The reorganization was effected by Quirinius, governor of Syria, who was also behind a new tax registration which led to an unsuccessful uprising fomented by Judas the Galilean, the founder of the Jewish revolutionary party of the Zealots. The extensive powers of Roman governors included the choice and dismissal of Jewish high priests. Unlike during the previous centuries, during the lifetime of Jesus most of these high priests installed by the Romans remained in office for only a short period, with the exception of Annas (AD 6–15) and Caiaphas (AD 18–36/7), to both of whom leading parts are assigned in the trial of Jesus. Under Roman surveillance, the Jewish high priest and his senate, the Sanhedrin, which acted as both council and tribunal, continued to play a significant role in the day-to-day government of Judaea and Jerusalem, whereas Galilee, the country of Jesus, enjoyed near complete independence under Herod Antipas as long as the taxes were duly delivered to Rome.

The public life of Jesus as a charismatic healer and teacher began in Galilee in the wake of the missionary activity of John the Baptist with whose message of repentance and proclamation of the approaching kingdom of God Jesus started his own preaching career. In the Gospel of Luke, John's mission is dated to the fifteenth year of the emperor Tiberius or AD 29. It was of short duration and ended with the beheading of the Baptist by order of Herod Antipas, ruler of Galilee, probably in the same year. The inauguration of Jesus' ministry must therefore also be placed in AD 29. The New Testament contains two views of the length of its duration. The Gospel of John, mentioning two or three Passovers, implies that it lasted at least three years. In the Synoptic Gospels, on the other hand, only one Passover and a single visit to Jerusalem are mentioned. This shorter chronology is historically the more likely. It is easier to explain why John, the most recent of the evangelists, felt the need to extend the period of the career of Jesus in order to accommodate his numerous and lengthy, almost certainly fictional speeches, rather than justifying its compression to less than twelve months, and possibly no more than six, by the three earlier evangelists. Before travelling to Jerusalem for the Passover pilgrimage, probably in AD 30, Jesus had been active in Galilee, in particular on the northern shore of the Lake of Gennesaret, with occasional short trips to the region of Tyre and Sidon in Lebanon and to the district of the Decapolis east of the Lake. Like most Galilean Passover pilgrims, he avoided the unfriendly land of the Samaritans and journeyed south along the Jordan valley passing through Jericho.

The Gospels differ on the circumstances of the execution of Jesus, but they unanimously assert that it happened at the end of a brief legal process or of two consecutive legal processes. Two types of law court functioned in first-century AD Palestine, whether under Roman or Herodian government. Jewish judges were always in charge of the administration of the law of Moses in conformity with the traditional regulations, but when Judaea came under direct Roman government, political matters were handled by the chief representative of the emperor, who, as a rule, was a high Roman civil servant. This governor bore the title of prefect between AD 6 and 41 and that of procurator from AD 44 to 66. In the intervening three years (AD 41–44) the Romans ceded all the governing powers to the Herodian-Jewish king Agrippa I.

Before investigating the two trial accounts contained in the Gospels, one before a Jewish court, as reported in the Synoptics, the other before Pilate's tribunal, it will be useful to outline the legal systems in force in Roman Judaea during the age of Jesus.

*The Roman provincial system*

Let us start with the Roman jurisdiction. The first-century Jewish historian Flavius Josephus (AD 37–c. 100) clearly states that at the moment of the introduction in AD 6 of direct Roman administration in Judaea, Coponius, the first prefect, arrived in Jerusalem, 'entrusted by Augustus with full powers, including the infliction of capital punishment' (*Jewish War* 2:117). This means that Pontius Pilate, who twenty years after Coponius came to occupy the office from AD 26 to 36, had absolute discretion regarding the fate of Jesus. Pilate had the authority to deal with him with all the severity of Roman law after Jesus had been charged with disloyalty to the emperor and the state. The normal penalty for the crime of sedition was crucifixion, reserved for foreigners, i.e. non-Roman citizens, as well as for bandits and slaves, and the governor personally had the right to inflict the appropriate punishment on such criminals. So the Roman side of the trial of Jesus, unlike that of Paul whose case was complicated by his claim of Roman citizenship, raises no legal or judicial problem of any kind. If Jesus was accused of revolutionary activity and was found guilty, Pilate had the right to crucify him. He was even duty-bound to do so.

*The biblical legal system*

The Jewish court proceedings and their relation to the legal competence of Rome are more complex. Hence in order to shed some light on the legal aspects of the Passion story it is necessary to glance at the juridical system directly inherited from Scripture by first-century Judaism.

On the lowest level, justice had been administered since biblical times by the elders of each locality, and the public venue of the hearings was the city gate. Punishment, including the death penalty, was imposed there and then after the examination of the cases in the presence of anyone wishing to attend (Dt 21:18–21; 22:13–21; 1 Kgs 21:11–13). But already during the time of the kings of Judah, before the first fall of Jerusalem in 586 BC, we encounter professional law officials, chosen by the Jewish kings to deal with offences. 'You shall appoint judges ... in all your towns and they shall judge the people with righteous judgement' (Dt 16:18). This new arrangement came into force as the result of the reform initiated by King Jehoshaphat in the middle of the ninth century BC. This king set up judges in all the major cities of the kingdom of Judah, as well as a special tribunal of priests in Jerusalem under the presidency of the high priest, to act as a kind of established appeal court, dealing with issues which exceeded the competence of provincial judges (2 Chron 19:4–11). Priestly supremacy in legal matters was codified in the legislation promulgated in the Book of Deuteronomy, which specifies that difficult legal matters, involving among other things assault and homicide, had to be dealt with by the supreme tribunal of 'the Levitical priests' in the capital city of Jerusalem (Dt 17:8–12).

In connection with the accounts of the trial of Jesus it must be remembered that according to biblical law, no court proceeding could take place unless trustworthy prosecution witnesses had proved that the accused had committed the offence or crime with which he was charged. Information about the stringent testing of witnesses is available in the apocryphal supplement attached to the Book of Daniel, dealing with Susannah and the wicked elders, and in the tractate of the Mishnah called Sanhedrin in rabbinic literature. In capital cases the testimony of two or three witnesses was required; no one could be convicted and put to death on the evidence of a single witness (Dt 17:6). When the execution was by stoning, the witnesses had to act also as executioners; they literally had to cast the first stones (Dt 17:7).

As far as capital sentences are concerned, the prohibition under pain of death of work on the Sabbath day (Ex 31:15) is illustrated in the Bible by the incident of a Jew caught gathering firewood in the wilderness on the day of sabbatical rest. The scriptural narrator reports that the unfortunate man was brought before Moses and Aaron, who ordered in

God's name that 'all the congregation [should] stone him with stones outside the camp' (Ex 31:32–6).

The Bible lists twelve categories of crime which carried the death penalty: (1) homicide (Ex 21:12; Lev 24:17; Num 35:16–21); (2) abduction of a man in order to sell him as a slave (Ex 21:16; Dt 24:7); (3) idolatry (Ex 22:19; Lev 20:1–5; Dt 13:2–19; 17:2–7); (4) blasphemy (Lev 24:15–16); (5) the breaking of the Sabbath (Ex 32:14–15; Num 15:32–6); (6) sorcery (Ex 22:17; Lev 20:27); (7) grave offences against parents (Ex 21:15, 17; Lev 20:8; Dt 21:18–21); (8) prostitution by a priest's daughter (Lev 21:9); (9) adultery (Lev 20:10; Dt 22:22); (10) incest (Lev 20:11–12, 14, 17); (11) male homosexual acts (Lev 20:13); and (12) bestiality (Lev 20:15–16). In the cases of the two gravest religious offences, idolatry and blasphemy, the prescribed form of execution was specifically by stoning.

Regarding the Jewish high court, which still functioned in Jerusalem in the first century AD, the Alexandrian Jewish philosopher Philo (c. 20 BC–c. AD 50) and the historian Flavius Josephus supply descriptions of great interest. Their accounts are very valuable for the understanding of the legal conditions which existed in the age of Jesus. Philo, interpreting Deuteronomy's depiction of the supreme court in Jerusalem, identifies the 'more discerning judges' with 'the priests and the head and leader of the priests', i.e. the Jewish high priest. In Philo's opinion, one of the commanding reasons for entrusting complicated cases to the high priest is that he was 'necessarily a prophet . . . and to a prophet nothing is unknown' (*Special Laws* 4:190–92). Josephus also defines the high priest and his colleagues as the officials whose task is to 'safeguard the laws, adjudicate in cases of dispute and punish those convicted of crimes' (*Against Apion* 2:194). The supreme court in Jerusalem consisted, according to the same author, of 'the high priest and the prophet and the council of the elders' (*Jewish Antiquities* 4:218). While during the existence of the kingdom of Judah the participation of a court prophet, an appointed royal functionary, in the decision of law cases is conceivable, by the time of Philo and Josephus a different interpretation was needed and the high priest, no doubt on account of his wearing the biblical instruments of divination (*Urim* and *Thummim*, Ex 28:30) affixed to his breastplate, was held to be endowed with prophetic perspicacity. A striking phrase in the Gospel of John echoes this understanding. The evangelist declares that Caiaphas, because he was the high priest, 'prophesied' when he was speaking of Jesus (Jn 11:49–52).

## Jewish law courts according to the Mishnah

The oldest rabbinic traditional law code, the Mishnah, has a special tractate called Sanhedrin, which contains a detailed account of the various Jewish tribunals and their procedural rules. The code itself was not written down before AD 200, by which time the great Sanhedrin of Jerusalem was no longer in existence. As a result, the acceptability and historical dependability of the information included in the Mishnah are hotly debated. Some features, like the attribution of the presidency of the court to the *Nasi* or chief rabbi instead of the high priest even before the destruction of the Temple, are patently incorrect. We know from the New Testament and Josephus that this was not so. The twist is due to the unwillingness of the rabbinic successors of the earlier Pharisees to accept that their opponents, the Sadducee chief priests, were *ex officio* in charge of the supreme tribunal. Nevertheless it is clear that apart from such 'religious-political' manipulations the tractate Sanhedrin preserves a number of legal traditions which are considerably older than AD 200. Some of these are likely to assist us when it comes to determining the reliability, or quite often the unreliability, of important particulars in the Gospel accounts of the Passion.

The Mishnah mentions three types of law court. At the lowest level stood the local tribunal competent to deal with run-of-the-mill civil cases (for example, who owes what to whom?). It consisted of three judges, or perhaps more exactly three arbitrators, and was probably not a standing body; each party designated his 'judge' for a given dispute and the two nominated judges coopted the third one.

The competence of the intermediate court, made up of twenty-three judges, covered criminal issues and even capital cases. This seems to have been a regional court. Originally these courts probably corresponded to the councils or synods established by the Roman governor of Syria, Gabinius, in the five districts into which he divided Palestine after it had been conquered by Pompey for Rome in 63 BC. Josephus lists Jerusalem and Jericho in Judaea, Sepphoris in Galilee, and Amathus in Transjordan as seats of such tribunals or Sanhedrins. The fifth place mentioned by him is Gadara, probably not a second city in Transjordan, but a third one in Judaea. Nevertheless it is possible that the name of the town, Gadara, is a mistake, in which case it should be corrected to read Adora, a place in Idumaea. If so, the southern region of the country would also be provided with its own tribunal (Josephus, *Jewish War* 1:169–70; *Jewish Antiquities* 14:91).

The Mishnah's supreme court, or the Great Sanhedrin of seventy-one judges, is located in Jerusalem. Its sessions were held in a special hall situated in the Temple area, the Hall of the Hewn Stone or *Lishkat ha-Gazit*. More than a tribunal, it was the senate of the Jewish people, its supreme judicial, legislative and administrative institution, three in one. In addition to dealing with major criminal cases, it was also empowered to declare war, change the boundaries of Jerusalem and the Temple, and above all to interpret the Law of Moses authoritatively. The Synoptic Gospels bring Jesus before this Sanhedrin, but at a meeting held not close to the Temple, but in the house of the high priest. The fact that the meeting entails the examination of witnesses and ends in Mark and Matthew by finding Jesus guilty of blasphemy, punishable by death, indicates that the evangelists envisage the 'council' (*synedrion*) as a tribunal, not simply as a consultative assembly.

As already established in connection with scriptural law, no accused person could be sentenced to death without the concurring testimony of at least two witnesses. It seems that in biblical times the witnesses could testify together, one being interrogated in the presence of the other, a condition which made the detection of false testimony more difficult. The apocryphal story of Susannah, mentioned earlier, represents a judicial innovation: the two elders, who jointly and mendaciously denounced Susannah as an adulteress, were separated and cross-examined singly by the wise judge Daniel. As a result, their testimony fell apart. One of them placed the sex incident under a mastic tree, whilst the other said that it happened under a yew tree. This discrepancy was sufficient to prove that the elders were liars. Consequently they, instead of Susannah, received the death penalty. The Mishnah sets out a list of circumstances on which the individually questioned witnesses had to agree. The absence of unanimous testimony is referred to in the account of the trial of Jesus by the Sanhedrin in the Gospels of Mark and Matthew. Only if the witnesses satisfied the court could the judges pursue the case further and reach a verdict. Each judge had to cast his vote, one after the other. Contrary to what we read in the Synoptics, no death sentence could be pronounced by common acclamation.

Every witness had to reassure the court about the due warning issued to the person who was on the point of committing a crime regarding the consequences of his action. The Bible enjoins that one should reprove one's neighbour in order to escape responsibility for shared guilt. The Mishnah expressly instructs judges specifically to inquire whether such a caution has been given. If not, the witnesses had to be disqualified. Was such a requirement in force in the age of Jesus? That it existed before the destruction of the Temple in AD 70 can be deduced from the Qumran Damascus Document, which makes formal warning a compulsory part of the legal procedure (9:2–9).

The need for the testimony of witnesses in capital cases is taken so literally that rabbinic law, codified in the Tosephta (third century AD), does not consider confession, that is, admission of guilt by the accused person, a sufficient ground for pronouncing a death sentence except in the specific case of secret propagation of idolatry, a crime which by nature was particularly difficult to prove. In all other cases conviction could follow only after the testimony of witnesses and after explicit warning (Tosephta Sanhedrin 11:1).

Another procedural rule of the Great Sanhedrin laid down that capital sentences could never be pronounced on the day of the court hearing itself; the decree of condemnation had to wait until the following day. 'Therefore trials involving death penalty may not be held *on the eve of sabbath or on the eve of a feast day*' (Mishnah Sanhedrin 4:1; Mishnah Betzah 5:2). That a court should not do business on a Sabbath is obvious. It is hardly surprising therefore that this is not expressly listed among the prohibited actions. In fact, since the proceedings had to be recorded by two court clerks, the Mishnah's prohibition to write as few as two letters on the Sabbath (Mishnah Shabbat 7:2) implicitly forbids the recording of minutes.

The issue is highly relevant to the assessment of the Passion account of the Synoptic Gospels. Some New Testament scholars are in principle unwilling to accept rabbinic literature as providing valid evidence for the age of Jesus. But if they object to the use of the Mishnah or the Tosephta because of the date of their redaction, they are not at liberty to reject first-century AD sources, such as Philo and the Dead Sea Scrolls. Philo writes: 'Let us not ... abrogate the laws laid down for its [the Sabbath's] observance and ... institute [on that day] proceedings in court' (*Migration of Abraham* 91). The Damascus Document from Qumran also firmly states that on the Sabbath day 'no one shall judge' (10:17–18).

## Death penalties

The Hebrew Bible recognizes two forms of death penalty. The most commonly used mode of execution was by judicial stoning (to be distinguished from lynch justice, the on-the-spot killing of someone by an outraged crowd). Persons found guilty of blasphemy (Dt 24:15–16), idolatry (Dt 17:2–7), Sabbath-breaking (Num 15:32–6), adultery and rape (Dt 22:22–4), etc. were put to death by stoning. The other death penalty explicitly listed is burning, reserved for certain sexual offences such as an attempt to contract marriage simultaneously with a woman and her mother (Lev 20: 14) or prostitution committed by a priest's daughter (Lev 21:9). The Mishnah (Sanhedrin 7:1) further refers to beheading by the sword, practised by the secular power, and to strangling.

All four forms were in use in the age of Jesus. Various stoning episodes appear in the New Testament itself: John 10:31–3 and 2 Corinthians 11:25 allude to failed attempts to stone Jesus and Paul; Acts 7:58 describes the execution of Stephen; and John 8:7 recounts Jesus' intervention which stopped the stoning of a woman caught in adultery. According to Josephus, James the brother of Jesus was executed by stoning (*Jewish Antiquities* 20:200). The Mishnah alludes to an actual case of burning the harlot daughter of a priest (Mishnah Sanhedrin 7:2) and, in a different context, Josephus relates that on his deathbed Herod the Great ordered the execution by fire of two teachers of the law and some of their students responsible for the removal of the decorative eagle that Herod had installed in the Temple (*Jewish War* 1:655). The later Herodian rulers, Antipas, Tetrarch of Galilee, and King Agrippa I, ordered the decapitation respectively of John the Baptist and the apostle James son of Zebedee (Mk 6:27; Acts 12:1). Strangulation as a legal method of execution described in the Mishnah seems to be a rabbinic innovation, but it was certainly in use during the reign of Herod the Great. Two of Herod's sons, Alexander and Aristobulus, were strangled in prison by order of the king and with the consent of the emperor Augustus (Josephus, *Jewish War* 1:547; *Jewish Antiquities* 16:394).

As regards crucifixion, since pre-exilic biblical times the hanging of the corpse of a criminal put to death by stoning was part of the execution ritual (Dt 21:22-3). The purpose of this cruel custom was to deter people from breaking the law. Actual crucifixion, or 'hanging a man alive on the tree' according to the Hebrew metaphor used in the Dead Sea Scrolls, was no longer attested as part of Jewish legal practice in the Herodian age, that is, from 37 BC onwards. Before Herod, however, the Maccabaean-Hasmonaean Jewish priest-king Alexander Jannaeus (103-76 BC) chose crucifixion for the punishment of 800 Pharisees who had rebelled against him and helped the invading Syrian Greek king Demetrius III. This is gruesomely described by Josephus (*Jewish War* 1:96-8; *Jewish Antiquities* 13:380-91) and is hinted at in the Qumran Nahum Commentary (4Q169 Nahum Commentary on Nahum 2:13). The utopian legislation contained in the Dead Sea Temple Scroll (64:6-13) also threatens traitors of the Jewish people with crucifixion.

Nevertheless, from the death of Herod the Great up to the fall of Jerusalem and Masada (from 4 BC to AD 73/74) the cross was the visible and tangible sign, indeed the hallmark, of the cruel presence of Rome in the Jewish lands. Having suppressed the rebellion which broke out after the death of Herod, Varus, the Roman governor of Syria, ordered the mass crucifixion of 2,000 Jewish revolutionaries in the Jerusalem area. The most dreadful cases occurred during the siege of Jerusalem (AD 70) when at one time up to 500 captured Jews were crucified by the Romans *every day.* We are told that there was not enough space in Jerusalem for the crosses and not enough crosses for the victims. Cruel Roman legionaries enjoyed beating and torturing the prisoners before crucifixion. In 1968 the bones of a first-century crucified Jew by the name of Yehohanan were discovered in Jerusalem. The nail is still fixed in the heel bones and the shinbones are broken.

For Christians the cross of Jesus is a unique phenomenon. For a first-century Jew it was a tragic everyday spectacle, but in Roman eyes it was insignificant, an unavoidable, if horrible, necessity. Crucifixion was a Roman speciality and Rome alone bore the responsibility for the crucified multitudes. Yet Cicero is fully justified when he calls it *crudelissimum teterrimumque supplicium*, the most cruel and abominable form of execution.

## C. The Temple authorities and Jesus

According to the Synoptic evangelists, Jesus provoked the hostility of the priestly authorities of the Temple almost immediately on his arrival in Jerusalem. Who were these authorities?

It goes without saying that the high priest occupied a leading position in Temple worship. Certain cult acts, such as entering the Holy of Holies of the sanctuary once a year on the Day of Atonement, was his exclusive privilege. He was also *ex officio* the president of the Great Sanhedrin or supreme court and principal doctrinal institution of Judaism. Moreover, the Romans treated him also as the civic and political chief of the Palestinian Jews. Josephus remarks: 'After the death of [Herod and the dismissal of Archelaus] the constitution became an aristocracy, and the high priests were entrusted with the leadership of the nation' (*Jewish Antiquities* 20:251). The high priest and his council were invested by the Roman governors of Judaea with the duty of safeguarding peace in the province and maintaining law and order, especially in the Temple, the most important meeting place in the city.

It would seem that because of his potential and often

very real influence, the Herodian and the Roman secular authority felt obliged to keep an eye on the high priest. This was done in a curious fashion. The pontifical office was surrounded by formalities, including the duty to wear the prescribed garments for the performance of certain functions. Therefore Herod the Great (37–4BC) and his successors, Agrippa I (AD 41–44) and Agrippa II (AD 50–c. 100), as well as the Roman governors during the intervening years, removed the ceremonial vestments of the high priest from the Temple and kept them under their own custody. It is hardly likely that they wished to interfere with the religious functions of the pontiff. The purpose of the move was political; the secular rulers intended to make it obvious to whom the ultimate authority belonged. The Roman governors of Judaea also desired to have prior knowledge of the high priest's plans (for example, his intention to convoke the Sanhedrin) for which, it must be surmised, the wearing of solemn robes was demanded by custom. On the occasion of religious feasts the vestments were delivered to the Temple seven days in advance. Meanwhile they were kept under lock and triple seal in the Antonia Fortress, next door to the Temple of Jerusalem (see Josephus, *Jewish Antiquities* 15:403–8; 18:93–4; 20:6–7).

The high priests were expected to collaborate with the secular power, and if they failed to do so, they were unceremoniously sacked. Herod the Great deposed the high priest Matthias son of Theophilus (5/4 BC) because of his involvement in the removal of the golden eagle from the Temple. The successor of Matthias, Joazar son of Boethus, was dismissed by Herod the Great's son, Archelaus, for supporting the popular revolt which broke out in 4 BC after the death of his father. Joazar was reinstated and first supported the census, which the Roman governor of Syria Quirinius implemented in Judaea in AD 6. Joazar then switched allegiance and toed the nationalist line, obliging Quirinius to depose him in favour of Annas (AD 6–15) of Gospel notoriety. Finally, when in AD 66 it became obvious that the war against Rome was unavoidable, the chief priests and the leading citizens of Jerusalem, representatives of the aristocratic peace party, wishing to prove their loyalty to the Romans, informed the procurator Florus of the failure of their efforts to pacify the people (Josephus, *Jewish War* 2:417–18).

Threats against the life of Jesus are occasionally recorded in the Gospels before the Passion, but they stand on flimsy ground or are based in John on much later Christian concepts anachronistically traced back to the lifetime of Jesus. Luke can hardly be believed when he asserts that the inhabitants of Nazareth attempted to murder Jesus for choosing Capernaum rather than his home town for the venue of his healing activity (Lk 4:23–30). The charges of Sabbath-breaking through charismatic healing or of blasphemy by Jesus calling God his Father are far-fetched, and in no circumstances can either of them be built up into a capital offence (Mk 3:6; Mt 12:14; Jn 5:18).

The real conflict between Jesus and the authorities stems in Mark, Matthew and Luke from the fateful incident which goes under the title of the cleansing of the Temple. In John the episode is placed in the beginning of the ministry of Jesus (Jn 2:13–21) and not in the last week of his life, and consequently has no impact on the Passion story. The Synoptic chronology, nevertheless, makes much better sense.

Mark, Matthew and Luke record that after his arrival in Jerusalem Jesus entered the Temple. There, we must deduce from what follows, he witnessed the goings-on in the busy merchants' quarter. Jesus, the rural holy man, was shocked by the hurly-burly of business in the Temple courtyard where sacrificial animals were sold, and by the noisy bargaining between money-changers and their clients, who had to convert ordinary currency into valuable silver drachms minted in Tyre, the only coins deemed suitable for sacred donations. Jesus decided there and then to put an end to these unholy dealings; he overturned the pigeon-vendors' stalls and the tables of the bankers and stopped all the wanderings in the holy place that buying and selling necessitated. The evangelists placed a combined quotation from the Bible in the mouth of Jesus: 'My house shall be called a house of prayer [Isa 56:7], but you have made it a den of robbers' (Jer 7:1), but this fits better with the need for biblical proof in the early Church than with the spontaneity of the style of teaching of Jesus (Mk 11:11–17; Mt 21:10–13; Lk 19:45–6).

A number of interpreters argue that this act of 'cleansing' was in fact a rebellion against the ritual worship in the sanctuary; that in fact Jesus was opposed to the Temple. There is a much simpler and more cogent interpretation, however. The holy northern provincial from Nazareth found intolerable what for the local people of Jerusalem and the officials was routine business required for the day-to-day and feast-to-feast running of the Temple. As had been pointed out earlier, this was Jesus' first visit to Jerusalem since he had become a public figure, and on the spur of the moment, the rural prophet allowed his hot Galilean blood to boil over. Naturally a noisy and tumultuous mayhem followed and the priestly guardians of law and order were bound to take notice. Not only did they resent the fact that their supremacy was spurned by a provincial upstart, they were also concerned that the creation of disorder in the Temple, with enormous crowds assembled there in Passover week, might bring about the violent intervention of the Romans. Jesus was a potential threat to peace in the same way as John the Baptist's eloquence was seen, according to Josephus, as a revolutionary threat, causing the powers that be to step in. According to Josephus this brought about the decapitation of John by the ruler of Galilee, Herod Antipas (*Jewish Antiquities* 18:118). Nevertheless, the chief priests did not intervene immediately because they apparently feared that any action against Jesus, held in high esteem by the people on account of his healing charisma, might seriously backfire against them and provoke a dangerous riot (Mk 11:18–19; Lk 19:47–8).

A second episode that testifies to the growing worry about Jesus on the part of the authorities is recorded by the Synoptic evangelists as occurring the following day. They relate that the day after the fracas in the Temple the chief priests, scribes and elders sent a deputation to Jesus. The envoys approached him when he was walking in the Temple, and sought to find out who had authorized him to 'do these things'. The phrase 'these things' can only refer to the brawl in the merchants' quarter. One can guess at the chief priests' line of thought: We did not commission you; who did? Jesus' purported reply was bound further to exasperate the already tense situation. He would answer the authorities only if they would tell him in public what they thought of John the Baptist. This was a clever trap in which the chief priests were bound to be caught. If they admitted that the Baptist was a messenger of God, Jesus would ask: Why did you not follow him then? On the other hand, if they denied that John was a prophet, the people, sympathetic to John, would be infuriated and might stone them. Their cowardly 'We do not know' elicited a triumphant 'If you don't know, I won't tell!' The Gospels make Jesus look very threatening (Mk 11:27–33; Mt 21:23–7; Lk 20:1–8).

The next move described in the Synoptics is the natural sequel to Jesus' challenge. The priestly guardians of order conceived an actual plot against him. The Synoptics date it two days before Passover, occurring in the palace of the high priest Caiaphas (Mt 26:3). The chief priests and the scribes met there and resolved to get rid of Jesus. However, they still lacked the courage to do so openly and face the music as they were afraid of widespread indignation because of the popularity of Jesus: 'Not during the feast, lest there be a tumult in the people.' The chief priests looked instead for an opportunity to arrest him by stealth on a later date (Mk 14:1–2; Mt 26:3–5; Lk 22:2).

In the Gospel of John, with its extended time-scale of the public life of Jesus, the enmity between him and the chief priests is depicted as of longer duration. It is attributed to the resentment felt by the representatives of officialdom at the sight of the charismatic activity of Jesus, which had recently culminated in the raising from the dead of his friend Lazarus (a person unknown to the Synoptics), an event described as having had wide repercussions in Jerusalem. Religious authority always looked with suspicious eyes on prophets performing miracles whose control was beyond their power. Without giving a precise date, John places the high-priestly plot against Jesus in the week before Passover. Alarmed by the enthusiasm surrounding Jesus, the chief priests, we are told, convoked the council. Jesus' success was seen as the likely cause of great popular excitement which the nervous, sword- and

spear-brandishing Romans might have mi[s]
signs of an imminent rebellion. Military int[e]
terrible consequences might follow. In the words
to the high priest, the Romans might come and
both our place (the Temple) and our nation'.

It was on that same occasion that the high p[r]
Caiaphas is said to have proclaimed, 'It is expedient [f]
you that one man should die for the people, and that the
whole nation should not perish' (Jn 11:45–52). As the official
in charge of the safeguard of the community, the pontiff
had to take precautionary measures. John makes Caiaphas
enunciate here an important Jewish legal principle, namely,
that the welfare of the community overrides the life of
an individual. The issue was repeatedly discussed by the
later rabbis. They had to determine what to do when the
Romans demanded the extradition of a Jewish revolutionary under the threat of indiscriminate reprisal against the
population of the town or village which was harbouring
the fugitive. The rabbis were generally unwilling directly
to hand over a Jew to Gentiles. However, in order to
protect the larger community, they attempted to persuade
the fugitive to give himself up of his own accord.

So from that moment on Jesus lived on borrowed time
although he still did not seem in imminent danger. For
even when the council met, the day before the eve of
Passover, the intervention of the authorities was planned
to take place only after the festival. No reason is given in
the Gospels for the sudden change of strategy. It must have
been the surprise treachery of Judas that struck the chief
priests as a godsend. Being experienced statesmen, they
grasped the opportunity without hesitation and sent in
their troops in the dead of night.

...es that follow I intend to sketch, interpret and, ...cessary, query the way the evangelists present to their readers the thirteen episodes of events that occurred during the final day of the life of Jesus of Nazareth, starting with the Last Supper and ending with his death and burial.

## 1. The Last Supper

Mk 14:17, 22—5
*And when it was evening he came with the twelve. And as they were eating, he took bread, and blessed and broke it, and gave it to them and said, 'Take; this is my body.' And he took the cup, and when he had given thanks he gave it to them, and they all drank of it. And he said to them, 'This is my blood of the covenant, which is poured out for many. Truly I say to you, I shall not drink again the fruit of the vine until the day when I drink it new in the kingdom of God.'*

Mt 26:20, 26—9
*When it was evening, he sat at table with the twelve disciples. Now as they were eating, Jesus took bread, and blessed and broke it, and gave it to the disciples and said, 'Take, eat, this is my body.' And he took the cup, and when he had given thanks he gave it to*

34

*them, saying, 'Drink of it, all of you; for this is my blood of the*
*covenant, which is poured out for many for the forgiveness of sins.*
*I tell you I shall not drink again this fruit of the vine until the*
*day when I drink it new with you in my Father's kingdom.'*

Lk 22:14–20
*And when the hour came, he sat at table, and the apostles with him.*
*And he said to them, 'I have earnestly desired to eat this Passover*
*with you before I suffer; for I tell you I shall not eat it until it is*
*fulfilled in the kingdom of God.' And he took a cup, and when he had*
*given thanks he said, 'Take this, and divide it among yourselves; for*
*I tell you that from now on I shall not drink the fruit of the vine*
*until the kingdom of God comes.' And he took bread, and when he*
*had given thanks he broke it and gave it to them, saying, 'This is*
*my body which is given for you. Do this in remembrance of me.'*
*And likewise the cup after the supper, saying, 'This cup which is*
*poured out for you is the new covenant in my blood.'*

Jn 13:1–2, 27–9
*Now before the feast of Passover ... during supper, the devil had*
*already put it into the heart of Judas Iscariot, Simon's son, to*
*betray him. ... Then after the morsel [given to Judas by Jesus],*
*Satan entered him. Jesus said to him, 'What you are going to do,*
*do quickly.' ... Some thought that, because Judas had the money*
*box, Jesus was telling him, 'Buy what we need for the feast' ...*

According to the time reckoning of the Jews the day begins
at dusk when the first stars become visible in the sky. So
the last day of the life of Jesus started in the evening of
what we would consider the previous day with his Last
Supper. A last dinner shared with the twelve apostles is
reported in all four Gospels, but the picture given by the
Synoptics differs greatly from John's version.

In the Fourth Gospel Jesus' Last Supper is given an extensive treatment. According to his habit, John inserts long speeches into his narrative on the '*new* commandment', which was not really new, of loving one another; on Jesus as the 'way' to the Father; on the Holy Spirit, and similar subjects. Jesus' humility is demonstrated in washing his apostles' feet, and the dinner ends with a magnificent prayer by Jesus for his followers (Jn 13–17). The event is not given a precise date beyond being placed '*before* the feast of Passover', but the subsequent narrative suggests that it happened at the start of 14 Nisan, the day before Jews celebrated the Passover, implying that this Last Supper was not a Passover meal. John's account contains no allusion to the institution of the Eucharist, but it makes clear that in the course of that supper Judas Iscariot, identified as 'Simon's son', made up his mind and left the company to betray Jesus. Some of the apostles apparently thought that Judas was sent by Jesus to purchase what was needed for the feast the following day (Jn 13:1–2, 21–31).

By contrast, the occasion is presented by the Synoptic evangelists as definitely a Passover dinner. It should be noted in passing that Passover could fall on any day of the week. In the morning of that day, the fourteenth day of the Jewish month of Nisan, the *eve* of the great feast, which was a Thursday, Jesus is reported as instructing his disciples to obtain and prepare the foodstuffs required by Jewish religious tradition for the celebration of the important ritual meal prescribed by the Bible. This included above all the Passover lamb, which was to be taken to the Temple where it would be ceremonially slaughtered by the priests. After sunset, at the start of 15 Nisan, Jesus reclined at table with his apostles and celebrated what is known in contemporary Judaism as the *Seder* meal. As the main dish, Jesus and his contemporaries ate roast lamb. In the course of this meal, during which unleavened bread was eaten and according to tradition four cups of wine were ritually blessed and drunk, the Synoptic evangelists report what is usually understood to be the institution of the Eucharist, the sacrament commemorating the Last Supper (Mk 14:12–21; Mt 26:17–25; Lk 22:7–14, 21–3). Thus the Eucharist is implicitly linked to the Passover in Mark and Matthew, and explicitly in Luke, where Jesus declares, 'I have earnestly desired to eat *this Passover* with you' (Lk 22:15). The three Gospels do not agree on the details of the ceremony. In particular, whereas neither Mark nor Matthew actually asserts that Jesus ordered the reiteration of the ritual, Luke adds, 'Do this in remembrance of me' (Lk 22:19). In this he is followed by, or more likely he follows, St Paul who, in his first letter to the Corinthians written in the mid-fifties AD, expressly claims that Jesus ordered the repetition of the ceremonial after both the bread and the cup (1 Cor 11:24–5). It is important to emphasize that all three evangelists refer to Jesus' vow of abstention from wine until the coming of the kingdom of God (Mk 14:25; Mt 26:29; Lk 22:18), with the implied meaning that he was not foreseeing his imminent death but was looking forward to the forthcoming completion of his divinely entrusted mission, the ushering in of God's everlasting reign.

At some stage during the supper, or immediately after it, Judas disappeared to do his deed, while Jesus and the eleven completed the ceremony by singing a hymn (Mk 14:26; Mt 26:30), no doubt the last of the Halleluiah Psalms (Pss 113–18) prescribed for that occasion. Having finished, the whole company headed out of the city towards a nearby orchard, known as Gethsemane (meaning oil press or valley of oil), on the Mount of Olives.

## 2. The arrest of Jesus

Mk 14:32, 43–50

*And they went to a place which was called Gethsemane ... And immediately, while he was still speaking, Judas came, one of the twelve, and with him a crowd with swords and clubs, from the chief priests and the scribes and the elders. ... And they laid hands on him and seized him. But one of those who stood by drew his sword, and struck the slave of the high priest and cut off his ear. And Jesus said to them, 'Have you come out as against a robber, with swords and clubs to capture me? Day after day I was with you in the temple teaching, and you did not seize me. But let the Scriptures be fulfilled.' And they all forsook him and fled.*

Mt 26:47–56

*Then Jesus went with them to a place called Gethsemane ... While he was still speaking, Judas came, and with him a great crowd with swords and clubs, from the chief priests and the elders of the people. ... Then they came up and laid hands on Jesus and seized him. And behold one of those who were with Jesus stretched out his hand and drew his sword, and struck the slave of the high priest, and cut off his ear. Then Jesus said to him, 'Put your sword back into its place; for all who take the sword will perish by the sword'. ... At that hour Jesus said to the crowds, 'Have you come out as against a robber, with swords and clubs to capture me? Day after day I sat in the temple teaching, and you did not seize me. But all this has taken place, that the Scriptures of the prophets might be fulfilled.' Then all the disciples forsook him and fled.*

Lk 22:47–53

*And when he came to the place.... While he was still speaking, there came a crowd, and the man called Judas, one of the twelve, was leading them.... And when one of those who were about him saw what would follow, they said, 'Lord, shall we strike with the sword?' And one of them struck the slave of the high priest and cut off his right ear. But Jesus said, 'No more of this!' and he touched his ear and healed him. Then Jesus said to the chief priests and officers of the temple and elders, who had come out against him, 'Have you come out as against a robber, with swords and clubs? When I was with you day after day in the temple, you did not lay hands on me. But this is your hour, and the power of darkness.'*

Jn 18:1–12

*When Jesus had spoken these words, he went forth with his disciples across the Kidron valley, where there was a garden which he and his disciples entered. Now Judas, who betrayed him, also knew the place; for Jesus often met there with his disciples. So Judas, procuring a band of soldiers and some officers from the chief priests and the Pharisees, went there with lanterns and torches and weapons.... Then Simon Peter, having a sword, drew it and struck the high priest's slave and cut off his right ear. The slave's name was Malchus. Jesus said to Peter, 'Put your sword into its sheath; shall I not drink the cup which the Father has given me?' So the band of soldiers and their captain and the officers of the Jews seized Jesus and bound him.*

John, who has abandoned the company of the Synoptics in the account of the Last Supper, rejoins them in the episode of the arrest of Jesus. He designates the venue as a garden across the Kidron valley, without calling it Gethsemane. But since for John this was not Jesus' first visit to Jerusalem, he can remark that the place had been regularly frequented by Jesus on previous occasions, and in consequence was known to Judas.

Jesus prayed there in the solitude, invoking God as '*Abba*', 'Father' or 'My Father'. The word is given in Aramaic in Mark and in Greek in Matthew and Luke. *Abba* is a familiar but also respectful expression. It is not the equivalent of 'Daddy', as some New Testament scholars have unwisely ventured to propose. It is one of the few words which have been preserved and transmitted by the evangelists in Jesus' mother tongue. While he was lost in prayer, his exhausted disciples could no longer keep their eyes open and fell asleep (Mk 14:26–42; Mt 26:30–46; Lk 22:39–46).

In the concise dramatic orchestration of the story the quiet rest is disturbed by the arrival of Judas and a group of armed men. The Synoptics and John are not wholly in agreement here. According to the former, the men were the law enforcers controlled by the chief priests and the elders who dispatched them to place Jesus under arrest. Luke, probably mistakenly as it is against all verisimilitude, reports that the chief priests, the officers of the Temple and their lay supporters, the elders, also accompanied Judas (Lk 22:52). There is a tendency in the Synoptics to assert the presence of these 'enemies' everywhere from the arrest of Jesus until his crucifixion. But nothing in the later story would support Luke's allegation.

John in turn speaks of the arrival of a contingent of soldiers, commanded by a fairly high-ranking officer as well as 'the officers of the Jews' (Jn 18:12). Is this a hint at Roman participation in the arrest of Jesus with the moral support of Jewish liaison officers? The matter will be given further consideration at a later stage. In John the super-natural superiority of Jesus is manifested through the soldiers falling to the ground when Jesus tells them that he is the man they are looking for.

The arrival of the police or soldiers triggered off a token armed resistance by one of the apostles, in the course of which a slave or servant of the high priest was wounded. In John, the anonymous disciple of the Synoptics becomes Simon Peter, the leader of the apostles, and the injured slave/servant is named Malchus. The wounded man was miraculously healed by Jesus in Luke, but not in the other two Synoptics or John. With the exception of Mark, who remains silent on the matter, the other evangelists present Jesus as opposed to violence. Surprisingly, the attacker was not held by the forces of order. At the end, only Jesus was detained against his verbal protest. John, but not the Synoptics, makes the policemen bind him before he is led away. His pusillanimous disciples, with one exception, abandoned him and ran (Mk 14:43–52; Mt 26:47–56; Lk 22:47–53).

The exception was Peter, the leader of the apostles, who inconspicuously followed Jesus to the courtyard of the high priest. But forgetting his loud protest that he would never betray his master, he showed himself to be a coward. He repeatedly denied that he was a follower of Jesus. And when his dialectal Aramaic revealed to the Judaeans that he was Galilean – the 'stupid' Galilean with a funny accent was a proverbial object of mockery in Jerusalem according to the rabbis – he still insisted that he did not even know him (Mk 14:53–4, 66–72; Mt 26:57–8, 69–75; Lk 22:54–62).

In sum, the four evangelists have handed down basically identical traditions apart from three instances. They differ on the date when the event was supposed to occur: before Passover in John, on the festival of Passover in the Synoptics. They also leave slightly ajar the door leading to the question of the identity of the members of the arresting party guided by Judas. Did legionaries take part in the raid or was it a purely Jewish affair? The third discrepancy concerns the next stage of the story: Jesus was taken in one direction according to John and in another according to the Synoptics.

### 3. The interrogation of Jesus according to John

Jn 18:13–14, 19–24

*First they led him to Annas; for he was the father-in-law of Caiaphas, who was high priest that year. It was Caiaphas who had given counsel to the Jews that it was expedient that one man should die for the people. . . . The high priest then questioned Jesus about his disciples and his teaching. Jesus answered him, 'I have spoken openly to the world; I have always taught in synagogues and in the temple, where all Jews come together; I have said nothing secretly. Why do you ask me? Ask those who have heard me, what I said to them; they know what I said.' When he had said this, one of the officers standing by struck Jesus with his hand, saying, 'Is that how you answer the high priest?' Jesus answered him, 'If I have spoken wrongly, bear witness to the wrong; but if I have spoken rightly, why do you strike me?' Annas then sent him bound to Caiaphas, the high priest.*

In John's narrative, the detachment of soldiers (*speira* or cohort) under the command of a tribune (a *chiliarchos*), together with 'the officers of the Jews', took Jesus to Annas, described as the high priest (Jn 18:19). Who was this Annas? John and Luke muddle the issue of the Jewish high priest-hood, although Luke's mistake occurs in an earlier section of his Gospel and is not repeated in the Passion account.

According to John, the high priest Annas was the father-in-law of Caiaphas, the high priest 'of that year'. In Luke's Gospel at the start of the public activity of John the Baptist, Annas and Caiaphas jointly hold the high priesthood (Lk 3:2). However, in virtue of the unanimous testimony of the Bible, Josephus, Philo and the rabbis, the pontifical office could be occupied only by a single incumbent. Also, there was no annual rotation in the high-priestly succession. The error of the evangelists stems from two likely sources. In the first century AD, and more precisely between the creation of the Roman province of Judaea in AD 6 and the outbreak of the first Jewish war against Rome sixty years later, there were eighteen holders of the high-priestly office. Of these Annas sat on the pontifical throne for nine years, Caiaphas for eighteen years and Ananias son of Nebebaeus for twelve years. This adds up to thirty-nine years. In other words, the remaining fifteen high priests lasted twenty-one years all told, which means that few of them held the post for as long as two years and some of them for less than one year.

The inquiry by Annas is presented as informal, without the presence of a council or the calling of witnesses. He was interested in Jesus' Galilean disciples and in his private teaching. While nothing is stated in plain words, the high priest seems to have angled for politically compromising words on the part of Jesus. Galileans had the reputation of being revolutionaries. But according to John, Jesus' main defence was that he had nothing to hide; he had been teaching openly in the Temple and had no secret agenda. In this account Jesus, instead of remaining silent, stands up for himself, and when an overzealous Jewish officer strikes him for being disrespectful to Annas, instead of offering the other cheek, he objects with dignity (Jn 18:23).

No other detail of the interrogation is given in John. All we learn is that Annas sent the prisoner, still bound, to the high priest Caiaphas. Since the Fourth Gospel contains no further proceedings against Jesus by the Jewish authorities, we must conclude that the subsequent decision by Caiaphas to deliver Jesus to the Romans was based on the report of the preliminary inquiry conducted by Annas.

## 4. The night trial of Jesus before the Sanhedrin

Mk 14:53, 55–65

*And they led Jesus to the high priest; and all the chief priests and the elders and the scribes were assembled. . . . Now the chief priests and the whole council sought testimony against Jesus to put him to death; but they found none. For many bore false witness against him, and their witness did not agree. And some stood up and bore false witness against him, saying, 'We heard him say, I will destroy this temple that is made with hands, and in three days I will build another, not made with hands.' Yet not even so did their testimony agree. And the high priest stood up in the midst, and asked Jesus, 'Have you no answer to make? What is it that these men testify against you?' But he was silent and made no answer. Again the high priest asked him, 'Are you the Christ, the Son of the Blessed?' And Jesus said, 'I am; and you will see the Son of man seated at the right hand of Power, and coming with the clouds of heaven.' And the high priest tore his garments, and said, 'Why do we still need witnesses? You have heard his blasphemy. What is your decision?' And they all condemned him as deserving death. And some began to spit on him, and to cover his face, and to strike him, saying to him, 'Prophesy!' And the guards received him with blows.*

Mt 26:57, 59–68

*Then those who had seized Jesus led him to Caiaphas the high priest, where the scribes and the elders had gathered. ... Now the chief priests and the whole council sought false testimony against Jesus that they might put him to death, but they found none, though many false witnesses came forward. At last two came forward and said, 'This fellow said, I am able to destroy the temple of God, and to build it in three days.' And the high priest stood up and said, 'Have you no answer to make? What is it that these men testify against you?' But Jesus was silent. And the high priest said to him, 'I adjure you by the living God, tell us if you are the Christ, the Son of God.' Jesus said to him, 'You have said so. But I tell you, hereafter you will see the Son of man seated at the right hand of Power, and coming on the clouds of heaven.' Then the high priest tore his robes, and said, 'He has uttered blasphemy. Why do we still need witnesses? You have now heard his blasphemy. What is your judgement?' They answered, 'He deserves death.' They then spat in his face, and struck him; and some slapped him, saying, 'Prophesy to us, you Christ! Who is it that struck you?'*

Lk 22:54, 63–5

*And then they seized him and led him away, bringing him into the high priest's house. ... Now the men who were holding Jesus mocked him and beat him; they also blindfolded him and asked him, 'Prophesy! Who is it that struck you?' And they spoke many other words against him, reviling him.*

Whilst in the Gospel of John Jesus is examined by Annas, in the Synoptic accounts the Jewish policemen take him directly to the house of the high priest, nameless in Mark and Luke, but identified as Caiaphas in Matthew, as in John too.

From the start, the story teems with difficulties.

Although the arrest of Jesus was sudden and unprepared, the evangelists declare that the whole august body of the Sanhedrin – consisting of seventy-one members according to the Mishnah – was already assembled in the high priest's palace at night, and on Passover night of all nights. Not only were the councillors present, but there was also a whole bunch of witnesses ready to testify against Jesus. Was all this carefully organized when it was still uncertain whether Jesus would actually be found let alone detained?

The harmony between the Synoptics immediately breaks down. Luke makes no mention of a nocturnal session of the Sanhedrin. If we now turn to Mark and Matthew, another oddity emerges. Although we are told that the authorities had decided in advance that Jesus must be eliminated (Mk 14:1; Mt 26:4; Lk 22:2), they carefully maintain the outward appearances of a due legal process. No one should be condemned without witnesses; so we are presented with witnesses for the prosecution. They are already there, waiting. They come forward and make their depositions, but although the judges seem to be interested only in conviction – Matthew even claims that the court was looking for *pseudomartyria* or *false* testimony (Mt 26:59) – the accusations are all rejected because, to quote Mark's sober comment, they 'did not agree'. When finally two witnesses stand up and proffer an identical charge, namely, that Jesus had issued threats against the Temple, the tribunal, abiding by the law governing testimony in capital cases, is still unsatisfied (Mk 14:55–9; Mt 26:59–61). This quibbling about minutiae is surprising and perhaps explains why Luke prefers to keep altogether silent about the witnesses.

After this punctilious adherence to the rules, one would have expected the dismissal of the case, but the evangelists suddenly change direction. First the high priest invites Jesus to respond to the charges, although they have already been dismissed. Not surprisingly, Jesus refuses to answer them. Next, Mark and Matthew assert that Caiaphas adopted the tactic of direct challenge and confronted Jesus with 'Are you the Christ, the Son of the Blessed?' – the 'Blessed' being a substitute name for God. The words can be paraphrased, 'Are you the Messiah, the promised royal deliverer of Israel?' In Jewish religious thought, before and after the age of Jesus, a king of the House of David, and above all the King-Messiah, was considered the 'Son of God' on the basis of Psalm 2:7, where on the occasion of the enthronement of the Israelite monarch, God declares: 'You are my son, today I have begotten you.' Elsewhere he also makes a promise to King Solomon: 'I will be his father, and he shall be my son' (2 Sam 7:14). Indeed, in the commonly used metaphorical terminology of Judaism 'Messiah' and 'Son of God' were interchangeable; they were synonyms.

Jesus' answer to the high priest's question varies in the Gospels. In Mark we are faced with a straight 'I am', but with a less direct 'You say that I am' in several important Mark manuscripts. Luke employs the same formula and Matthew has 'You have said so.' The indirect style, which seems to have been Jesus' favourite way of speaking about himself, is equivocal; theoretically it can be understood as either yes or no. However, the expression is found with a definitely negative connotation in rabbinic literature: 'You have said it' is tacitly paraphrased 'You, not I', meaning 'I would disagree, or at least I would not put it that way.'

Nevertheless Jesus' answer was taken by the high priest and the judges as a plain admission not only in Mark, but also in Matthew and Luke who use ambiguous formulas.

Combined with Jesus' further comment about the 'Son of man [being] seated on the right hand of the Power and coming with the clouds of heaven', a description of the triumphal revelation of the Messiah at the end of time, his words without any further inquiry were judged by the high priest as blasphemous. Caiaphas then suddenly reverted to ceremonial orthodoxy. We are told that he rent his garments, as required by rabbinic law. Then he and all the members of the Sanhedrin pronounced a unanimous verdict of guilty. Jesus had committed blasphemy and therefore deserved the death penalty. But the fundamental question is whether Jesus' words, supposing that he actually uttered them, can be construed as amounting to the capital crime of blasphemy.

Strangely, the Sanhedrin breathes no word about execution. Biblical law, as we have seen, prescribes stoning as the punishment for blasphemy, and the New Testament itself and Josephus report that it was in practice in the age of Jesus. Instead, the case is transferred without any explanation to a different jurisdiction, that of the Roman governor of Judaea.

The pronouncement of the capital sentence was accompanied by abuse and mocking of the prisoner Jesus. Mark and Matthew insinuate that the perpetrators were the judges themselves: 'And they all condemned him as deserving death. And some began to spit on him', etc. They were playing the prophet game in which the blindfolded Jesus was beaten and asked to 'prophesy' who had hit him (Mk 14:60–65; Mt 26:62–7). According to Mark, the policemen also joined the magistrates and the dignified courtroom was transformed into a scene of pandemonium. Luke also reports the mockery and ill-treatment of Jesus, but attributes them with greater verisimilitude to the guards who were holding him during the night, prior to his arraignment before the court the following morning (Lk 22:63–5). Luke elsewhere notes that Herod Antipas' soldiers also poked fun at Jesus (Lk 23:11). Finally, a scene of scoffing by Roman legionaries follows the scourging of Jesus (Mk 15:16–20; Mt 27:27–31). Some of these incidents could well be duplicates.

In sum, the reliability of the account of Jesus' appearance before the Sanhedrin and his condemnation to death is seriously undermined by the repeated contradictions and historical and legal improbabilities of Mark's account, which has been copied in substance by Matthew. Luke and John further muddy the waters. John ignores any trial of Jesus by a Jewish court and Luke omits the night session of the Sanhedrin. However, the four evangelists are once more reunited in their report of the events which occurred the following morning.

## 5. The morning meeting of the Sanhedrin

Mk 15:1
*And as soon as it was morning the chief priests with the elders and the scribes, and the whole council held a consultation; and they bound Jesus and led him away and delivered him to Pilate.*

Mt 27:1–2
*When morning came, all the chief priests and the elders of the people took counsel against Jesus to put him to death; and they bound him and led him away and delivered him to Pilate, the governor.*

Lk 22:66–23:1

*When day came, the assembly of the elders of the people gathered together, both chief priests and scribes; and they led him away to their council, and they said, 'If you are the Christ, tell us.' But he said to them, 'If I tell you, you will not believe; and if I ask you, you will not answer. But from now on the Son of man shall be seated at the right hand of the Power of God.' And they all said, 'Are you the Son of God then?' And he said to them, 'You say that I am.' And they said, 'What further testimony do we need? We have heard it ourselves from his lips.' Then the whole company of them arose, and brought him before Pilate.*

Jn 18:28

*Then they led Jesus from the house of Caiaphas to the praetorium. It was early. They themselves did not enter the praetorium so that they might not be defiled, but might eat the Passover.*

John, let it be repeated, mentions no meeting of the chief priests and their council. Jesus is simply dispatched from the house of the high priest to the *praetorium*, Pilate's Jerusalem residence in the palace of Herod. The time is defined: it happened early in the morning of the eve of Passover, 14 Nisan, definitely *before* the Passover supper.

The three Synoptic evangelists describe a gathering of the members of the Sanhedrin in the morning of Passover day. This meeting, the second in Mark and Matthew and the only one in Luke, is called a consultation. We are not told whether Jesus was present and absolutely no detail of the discussion is given. Only the final resolution of the court is revealed, namely, that the prisoner Jesus should be bound and transferred to the tribunal of Pontius Pilate (Mk 15:1; Mt 27:1–2; Lk 22:66–23:1). Although it is not explicitly admitted, it becomes clear from what follows that the Sanhedrin suddenly changed tack. During the night the alleged messianic claim of Jesus was treated as a religious offence; in the morning, like a chameleon, blasphemy changed its colours and was conveniently metamorphosed into a political offence, anti-Roman revolutionary activity. However, none of the evangelists specifies in advance the indictment that the chief priests are to present to Pilate. The unformulated charge will come into the open through the question addressed by the governor to Jesus. By any standard this sweeping change of tactics would require some explanation, for instance that a new political accusation acceptable to Pilate was necessary because the Sanhedrin lacked the power to sentence and execute Jesus for blasphemy. However, no such justification is given.

Luke, who follows a tradition in which there is no night trial of Jesus, having acquainted himself with the version of Mark and/or of Matthew, attempts here to combine their account with his own morning-only Sanhedrin meeting. He ascribes the question about the Messiahship of Jesus not to the high priest, as do Mark and Matthew, but to the judges ('they said'), and follows it up with an evasive reply from Jesus: It is not worth answering as the court will not believe anything he may say. Then Luke reproduces from Mark and Matthew the abridged version of Jesus' statement about the Son of man sitting on the right hand of God. Significantly, while in Luke the Sanhedrin declares the saying of Jesus to be a confession of guilt, it pronounces no sentence of condemnation, nor does it refer to the death penalty (Lk 22:63–5, 67–71).

In short, in Luke's tradition there is only a morning meeting of the council without witnesses: Jesus' words are declared as evidence of his guilt but are not qualified as blasphemous and the court passes no judgement. What is common to all four Gospels is the decision to deliver Jesus to the Roman authority.

## 6. The suicide of Judas

Mt 27:3–10
*When Judas, his [Jesus'] betrayer, saw that he was condemned, he repented and brought back the thirty pieces of silver to the chief priests and the elders, saying, 'I have sinned in betraying innocent blood.' They said, 'What is that to us? See to it yourself.' And throwing down the pieces of silver in the Temple, he departed and he went and hanged himself. But the chief priests, taking the pieces of silver, said, 'It is not lawful to put them into the treasury, since they are blood money.' So they took counsel, and bought with them the potter's field, to bury strangers in. Therefore that field has been called the Field of Blood to this day. Then was fulfilled what had been spoken by the prophet Jeremiah, saying, 'And they took the thirty pieces of silver, the price of him on whom a price had been set by some of the sons of Israel, and they gave them for the potter's field, as the Lord directed.'*

Matthew inserts a brief interlude about Judas between the trial of Jesus by the Sanhedrin and the transfer of the case to Pilate. He makes the traitor repent and return the bribe. The evangelists are innocent of modern speculations about Judas' higher motives such as his wish to catapult Jesus into revealing his concealed Messiahship. No clear time of the event is given. According to Matthew the trial of Jesus took place in the house of Caiaphas, but Judas' meeting with the chief priests and elders is located in the Temple, a different venue no doubt on a different occasion.

As the priestly authorities refused to take back the money, Judas threw it away and in despair hanged himself. The rest of the story has all the appearances of a folk tale artificially combined with a scriptural citation to turn the event into the fulfilment of a prophecy. Left with an unpleasant dilemma – what to do with the returned blood money unfit for the Temple treasure – the chief priests decided to buy with it a field for the burial of strangers. There was a plot of land in Jerusalem known as the 'Field of Blood', and early Christian tradition associated it with the misadventure of Judas. The prophetic aspect of the incident is largely manufactured by Matthew. The quotation is said to be of Jeremiah, but it is invented or is more exactly a garbled mixture of Zechariah 11:12–13 and Jeremiah 18:2–3, 36:6–15. It is impossible to discern in the biblical excerpts even a remote connection with the Judas episode. Here, as in many other places, Matthew endeavours to portray the Passion story, disturbing for believers and unattractive for would-be converts, as a sequence of prophetically foretold and therefore providentially predestined events.

## 7. Jesus before Pilate

Mk 15:2–5
*And Pilate asked him, 'Are you the King of the Jews?' And he answered him, 'You have said so.' And the chief priests accused him of many things. And Pilate again asked him, 'Have you no answer to make? See how many charges they bring against you.' But Jesus made no further answer so that Pilate wondered.*

Mt 27:11–14

*Now Jesus stood before the governor; and the governor asked him, 'Are you the King of the Jews?' Jesus said, 'You have said so.' But when he was accused by the chief priests and elders, he made no answer. Then Pilate said to him, 'Do you not hear how many things they testify against you?' But he gave them no answer, not even to a single charge; so that the governor wondered greatly.*

Lk 23:2–5

*And they began to accuse him saying, 'We found this man perverting our nation, and forbidding us to give tribute to Caesar, and saying that he himself is Christ a king.' And Pilate asked him, 'Are you the King of the Jews?' And he answered him, 'You have said so.' And Pilate said to the chief priests and the multitudes; 'I find no crime in this man.' But they were urgent, saying, 'He stirs up the people, teaching throughout all Judea, from Galilee even to this place.'*

Jn 18:29–38

*So Pilate went out to them and said, 'What accusation do you bring against this man?' They answered him, 'If this man were not an evildoer, we would not have handed him over.' Pilate said to them, 'Take him yourselves and judge him by your own law.' The Jews said to him, 'It is not lawful for us to put any man to death.' This was to fulfil the word which Jesus had spoken to show by what death he was to die. Pilate entered the praetorium again and called Jesus, and said to him, 'Are you the King of the Jews?' Jesus answered, 'Do you say this of your own accord, or did others say it to you about me?' Pilate answered, 'Am I a Jew? Your own nation and the chief priests have handed you over to me; what have you done?' Jesus answered, 'My kingship is not of this world; if my kingship were of this world, my servants would fight that I might not be handed over to the Jews; but my kingship is not of*

*the world.' Pilate said to him, 'So you are a king?' Jesus answered,*
*'You say that I am a king. For this I was born, and for this I have*
*come into the world, to bear witness to the truth. Every one who*
*is of the truth hears my voice.' Pilate said to him, 'What is truth?'*
*After he had said this, he went out to the Jews again, and told*
*them, 'I find no crime in him.'*

As has been noted, in the morning session of the Sanhedrin, no mention is made by Mark and Matthew of the charge to be levelled against Jesus. We must conclude, however, in the light of the governor's question, 'Are you the King of the Jews?' that the indictment concerned Jesus' royal and messianic claim, namely, that he pretended to be the King-Messiah (Mk 14:2–5; Mt 27:11–14). Luke is more specific. He makes the Jewish representatives explicitly accuse Jesus of sedition: he assumes the royal title of the Christ, perverts the nation, and, worst of all from the Roman point of view, forbids the payment of taxes to the emperor. The latter accusation is, of course, diametrically opposed to the words earlier attributed to Jesus by all the Synoptics, including Luke. His saying about the tax money, 'Render to Caesar the things that are Caesar's', is the characteristic utterance not of a revolutionary, but of an apolitical teacher (Mk 12:17; Mt 22:21; Lk 20:25).

To Pilate's straight question whether he was the King of the Jews Jesus gives his customary noncommittal answer: 'You have said so.' And if the testimony of the Synoptics is accepted, he simply refused to reply to the many further accusations heaped on him by the chief priests.

In John the main lines of the account of Jesus' encounter with Pilate are the same, but there are also some notable variants. John depicts Pilate, to whom Jesus was probably presented at short notice, as obliging and cooperative.

He receives the chief priests early in the morning and, respectful of their purity concerns, meets them outside his residence. He politely inquires about the reason of their coming: 'What accusation do you bring against this man?' The Jewish delegation is described as cagey and in a hurry. No doubt they had many pressing matters to attend to in preparation for Passover. On that same afternoon the Temple was to become a giant slaughterhouse where priestly butchers would kill the thousands of Passover lambs for the *Seder* supper. And there were the preparations for the solemn ritual of the fifteenth day of Nisan, which the chief priests had to conduct. It consisted, Josephus tells us, of the sacrifice of two bulls, a ram and seven lambs to serve as burnt offerings, and a kid for sin offering (*Jewish Antiquities* 3:249). So when Pilate asks about the charges against Jesus, he is curtly told that the accused is a wrongdoer; otherwise they would not have brought him here. To this Pilate sensibly retorts – and John's Pilate is even more sensible than the Pilate of the Synoptics – that if the chief priests have nothing against him that concerns Rome, they should try him themselves according to Jewish law. This reply gives rise to a totally unexpected riposte, which grotesquely amounts to a tutorial on Roman law given by the Jewish delegation to the Roman prefect. He should know that the Romans have deprived the Sanhedrin of the right to pronounce and execute capital sentences: 'It is not lawful for us to put any man to death.' This extraordinary statement will be examined later. John's Pilate takes the reproof in his stride and meekly agrees to handle the case. So Jesus is ordered inside the palace, and the governor focuses his inquiry on Jesus' kingship. Pilate is told that it is spiritual, not of this world, John informs us. Pilate then concludes that the priestly leaders are trying to involve him in a theological dispute about something he would have called their *superstitio*, and impresses on them that religious matters are outside his sphere of competence and that he can find no crime in Jesus in the political domain.

At this juncture the evangelists, like virtuoso wizards, present their readers with a surprise, the unforeseen legal custom (or fiction) of the *privilegium paschale*, or Passover amnesty.

## 8. Jesus sent to Herod Antipas and back to Pilate

Lk 23:6–11

*When Pilate heard this, he asked whether the man was Galilean. And when he learned that he belonged to Herod's jurisdiction, he sent him over to Herod, who was himself in Jerusalem at that time. When Herod saw Jesus he was very glad, for he had long desired to see him, because he had heard about him, and he was hoping to see some sign done by him. So he questioned him at some length; but he made no answer. The chief priests and the scribes stood by, vehemently accusing him. And Herod with his soldiers treated him with contempt and mocked him; then, arraying him in gorgeous apparel, he sent him back to Pilate. Pilate then called together the chief priests and the rulers of the people and said to them, 'You brought me this man as one who was perverting the people; and after examining him before you, behold, I did not find this man guilty of any of your charges against him; neither did Herod, for he sent him back to us. Behold, nothing deserving death has been done by him; I will therefore chastise him and release him.'*

In Luke's special version of the dialogue between Pontius Pilate and the chief priests, two passing references deserve further attention. First, the chief priests are said to be accompanied by 'the multitudes'. No such large crowd has been mentioned before; who are they and where have they come from? John's account implicitly echoes Luke's and even enlarges on it. The delators of Jesus are no longer just the chief priests, but the chief priests and the whole nation, or simply 'the Jews'.

Second, Jesus is portrayed by his accusers as a mischief-maker who has been fomenting trouble 'from Galilee' to Jerusalem. The reminder that Jesus is Galilean provides Pilate with an opportunity to hand over a case which he does not fancy to the ruler of Galilee. Herod would understand everything so much better. In similar circumstances, we find another Roman governor, Festus, seeking King Agrippa II's help for formulating the charges against St Paul which would then be transmitted to the emperor Nero (Acts 25:24–7). Very conveniently Herod Antipas, no doubt trying to please the Jewish citizens of his realm, travelled to Jerusalem to attend, or to be seen to attend, the celebration of the Passover. Apparently he welcomed the chance given him by Pilate to make the acquaintance of Jesus. However, Jesus remained silent throughout the whole episode, as he was silent before Pilate, despite the many questions of the Herodian prince. He also refused to answer the renewed accusations of the chief priests and scribes, who followed him to the residence of Antipas. Herod's patience ran out with the tiresome prophet, and after allowing his soldiers to make fun of him and clothe him in royal garments, he politely returned Jesus to Pilate (Lk 23:2–12).

Luke's episode makes the already tight time schedule even tighter. The chief priests left the *praetorium* when Pilate had decided to hand the case over to Antipas and followed Jesus. They were then summoned again by the governor to resume the proceedings. In Luke all this is supposed to happen on Passover day. On returning to the governor's palace, the priests are told that having been found innocent by both Pilate and Herod, Jesus was going to be released, but not without a good beating to remind him of the advisability of staying on the straight and narrow path. As we shall see, flogging could be a preliminary to crucifixion, but it could also be inflicted on its own as a warning. The gesture seems to be intended to appease the chief priests; they would not be sent away without the feeling of having achieved at least something.

## 9. The Passover amnesty and Barabbas

Mk 15:6–11
*Now at the feast he used to release for them one prisoner for whom they asked. And among the rebels in prison, who had committed murder in the insurrection, there was a man called Barabbas. And the crowd came up and began to ask Pilate to do as he was wont to do for them. And he answered them, 'Do you want me to release for you the King of the Jews?' For he perceived that it was out of envy that the chief priests had delivered him up. But the chief priests stirred up the crowd to have him release for them Barabbas instead.*

Mt 27:15–20
*Now at the feast the governor was accustomed to release for the crowd one prisoner whom they wanted. And they had then a notorious prisoner called Barabbas. So when they had gathered, Pilate said to them, 'Whom do you want me to release for you, [Jesus] Barabbas or Jesus who is called Christ?' For he knew that*

*it was out of envy that the chief priests had delivered him up. Besides, while he was sitting on the judgement seat, his wife sent word to him, 'Have nothing to do with that righteous man, for I have suffered much over him today in a dream.' Now the chief priests and the elders persuaded the people to ask for Barabbas and destroy Jesus.*

Lk 23:17–19
*Now he was obliged to release one man to them at the festival. But they all cried out together, 'Away with this man and release to us Barabbas' – a man who had been thrown into prison for an insurrection started in the city, and for murder.*

Jn 18:39–40
*'But you have a custom that I should release one man for you at the Passover; will you have me that I release for you the King of the Jews?' They cried out again, 'Not this man, but Barabbas!' Now Barabbas was a robber.*

The surprise slant introduced into the Passion narrative by all the evangelists is the *Paschal privilege*, which entails the granting of reprieve to a Jewish prisoner held by the governor on the occasion of the feast of Passover. It is unheard of outside the Gospels and the Gospels themselves offer substantially different versions of the usage.

Some important manuscripts of Luke and the Gospel of John assert that the proclamation of amnesty at the festival was the Roman governor's duty. Mark and Matthew, in their turn, describe the amnesty as the governor's custom, but add a most unlikely detail: the reprieve was to be open-ended and the Jewish crowd could choose any detainee they desired. We are also faced with compromise solutions. Pontius Pilate himself proposes a choice between two named individuals, Jesus or Barabbas (Matthew), or he selects his preferred beneficiary, but the people attempt to bargain for another: 'I will let the King of the Jews go,' proposes the governor; 'No, we want Barabbas,' shout the crowds (Luke).

The manner of offering the alternatives may be confused, but the outcome is invariably the same. When invited to choose between a certain Barabbas, or Jesus Barabbas according to some manuscripts, and Jesus surnamed the Christ, the Jewish populace, persuaded by the chief priests (Mark and Matthew), not only demands the release of Barabbas, but also preposterously clamours for the crucifixion of Jesus. It is hard, indeed almost impossible, to imagine a nationalist Jewish crowd encouraging the Romans to kill one of their countrymen. Of Barabbas nothing is known outside the New Testament. John calls him a robber, a *lêstês* in Greek, a word regularly applied to Jewish revolutionaries or Zealots in Josephus. The Gospels imply that he was held in prison for his participation in a failed insurrection in Jerusalem in the course of which someone was murdered, no doubt by Barabbas (Lk 23:25). An odd candidate for prefectorial clemency, one would say. Some New Testament scholars, desirous to maintain the historicity of the Barabbas episode, point out that another governor, Albinus (AD 62–4), released Jewish prisoners on his arrival in Jerusalem. But from a closer reading of Josephus it appears that the pardon was selective. Criminals who deserved to be put to death were executed, and amnesty was extended only to people gaoled for petty offences (*Jewish Antiquities* 20:215). Barabbas was not the kind of person a Roman administrator would have felt at liberty in ordinary circumstances to let loose in a turbulent country. But maybe the circumstances were not normal on that particular Passover?

## 10. The death sentence

Mk 15:12–20

*And Pilate again said to them, 'Then what shall I do with the man whom you call the King of the Jews?' And they cried out again, 'Crucify him.' And Pilate said to them, 'Why, what evil has he done?' But they shouted all the more, 'Crucify him.' So Pilate wishing to satisfy the crowd, released for them Barabbas; and having scourged Jesus, he delivered him to be crucified. And the soldiers led him away inside the palace (that is, the praetorium); and they called together the whole battalion. And they clothed him in a purple cloak, and plaiting a crown of thorns they put it on him. And they began to salute him, 'Hail, King of the Jews!' And they struck his head with a reed, and spat upon him, and they knelt down in homage to him. And when they had mocked him, they stripped him of the purple cloak, and put his own clothes on him. And they led him out to crucify him.*

Mt 27:21–31

*The governor again said to them, 'Which of the two do you want me to release for you?' And they said, 'Barabbas.' Pilate said to them, 'Then what shall I do with Jesus who is called the Christ?' They all said, 'Let him be crucified.' And he said, 'Why, what evil has he done?' But they shouted all the more, 'Let him be crucified.' So when Pilate saw that he was gaining nothing, but rather that riot was beginning, he took water and washed his hands before the crowd, saying, 'I am innocent of this man's blood, see to it yourselves.' And all the people answered, 'His blood be on us and on our children!' Then he released Barabbas, and having scourged*

*Jesus, he delivered him to be crucified. Then the soldiers of the governor took Jesus into the praetorium, and they gathered the whole battalion before him. And they stripped him and put a scarlet robe upon him, and plaiting a crown of thorns they put it on his head, and put a reed in his right hand. And kneeling before him they mocked him, saying, 'Hail, King of the Jews!' And they spat upon him, and took the reed and struck him on the head. And when they had mocked him, they stripped him of the robe, and put his own clothes on him, and led him away to crucify him.*

Lk 23:20–24
*Pilate addressed them once more, desiring to release Jesus, but they shouted out, 'Crucify, crucify him!' A third time he said to them, 'Why, what evil has he done? I have found in him no crime deserving death; I will therefore chastise him and release him.' But they were urgent, demanding with loud cries that he should be crucified. And their voice prevailed. So Pilate gave sentence that their demand should be granted. He released the man who had been thrown into prison for insurrection and murder, whom they asked for; but Jesus he delivered up to their will.*

Jn 19:1–16
*Then Pilate took Jesus and scourged him. And the soldiers plaited a crown of thorns, and put it on his head, and arrayed him in a purple robe; they came up to him, saying, 'Hail, King of the Jews!' and struck him with their hands. Pilate went out again, and said to them, 'See, I am bringing him out to you, that you may know that I find no crime in him.' So Jesus came out, wearing the crown of thorns and the purple robe. Pilate said to them, 'Behold the man!' When the chief priests and officers saw him, they cried out, 'Crucify him, crucify him!' Pilate said to them, 'Take him yourselves and crucify him, for I find no crime in him.' The Jews answered him, 'We have a law, and by that law he ought to die, because he has*

*made himself the Son of God.' When Pilate heard these words, he was the more afraid; he entered the praetorium again and said to Jesus, 'Where are you from?' But Jesus gave no answer. Pilate therefore said to him, 'You will not speak to me? Do you not know that I have power to release you, and power to crucify you?' Jesus answered him, 'You would have no power over me unless it had been given you from above; therefore he who delivered me to you has the greater sin.' Upon this Pilate sought to release him, but the Jews cried out, 'If you release this man, you are not Caesar's friend; everyone who makes himself a king sets himself against Caesar.' When Pilate heard these words, he brought Jesus out and sat down on the judgement seat at a place called The Pavement, and in Hebrew, Gabbatha. Now it was the Day of Preparation of the Passover; it was about the sixth hour. He said to the Jews, 'Behold your King!' They cried out, 'Away with him, away with him, crucify him!' Pilate said to them, 'Shall I crucify your King?' The chief priests answered, 'We have no king but Caesar.' Then he handed him over to them to be crucified.*

After all the efforts deployed by the evangelists to exonerate Pilate, he is finally allowed to bring the proceedings to an unhappy conclusion by giving in, against his better judgement, to the repeated and increasingly furious Jewish demands. Barabbas was freed and Jesus was sentenced to be crucified. Pilate further instructed the soldiers to administer the scourging customary prior to execution (Mk 15:6–15; Mt 27:15–26). In Luke the flogging is only a bargaining ploy suggested by Pilate to the Jews – I will chastise him before releasing him – but nowhere does this evangelist say that his offer was accepted, let alone implemented (Lk 23:13–25).

In John the flogging appears to be Pilate's final stratagem to save Jesus. He hoped that the sight of the tortured man would make his accusers relent. But the Jewish crowd is becoming more furious and threatening. They would denounce Pilate as someone neglecting his duty to protect the interest of the emperor. Pilate, who could have put them to flight by a discreet hand-signal to his legionaries, is portrayed as frightened, and lets the Jews have their way. He sat on the judgement seat and handed Jesus over to them to be crucified. 'To them' is equivocal: it no doubt means the soldiers, but in the spirit of the Gospel it applies also and very particularly to the Jews.

Mark and Matthew insert here another scene of mockery of the prisoner, this time by the Roman soldiers (Mk 15:16–20; Mt 27:27–31), similar to the episode attributed by Luke to the Jewish policemen during the night after his arrest, and to Herod Antipas and his soldiers (Lk 22:63–6; 23:11), or to the insults and beatings of Jesus by the judges and the guards following his night trial and condemnation by the Sanhedrin for blasphemy (Mk 14:63–5; Mt 26:67–8). Again the derision of Jesus by the Roman soldiers after the death sentence pronounced by Pilate, recounted by Mark and faithfully repeated by Matthew (Mk 15:16–20; Mt 27:27–31), is omitted by Luke. Or perhaps more exactly Luke moved it to the scene of crucifixion, with the executioners jibing at Jesus and inviting the King of the Jews to save himself (Lk 23:35).

It may be of interest to recall here the yobbish horseplay described by Philo which took place in Alexandria on the occasion of the visit to the city by the Jewish Herodian king Agrippa I (*Flaccus* 36–40). The Greek crowd, intent on ridiculing the Jewish king, dressed a lunatic called Carabas in mock royal garments with a papyrus crown and a sceptre, provided him with a bodyguard, and gave him comic salute before beating him up. An attempt to link

Carabas to Barabbas has been advanced by some scholars, but it seems far-fetched.

Matthew appends three special supplements to Mark's account. First, Pilate is warned by his wife, who having had a nightmarish dream about Jesus urges her husband to have nothing to do with 'that righteous man' (Mt 27:19). Second, before sentencing Jesus to die on the cross, the governor protests his own, and symbolically the Romans' innocence, by washing his hands in public of the blood guilt of Jesus. Third, in addition to exculpating Rome, Matthew wishes to put the responsibility for the murder of Jesus fair and square on the whole Jewish race, present and future, by making 'all the people' cry out 'His blood be on us and on our children!' (Mt 27:24–5).

## II. The crucifixion

Mk 15:21–32

*And they compelled a passer-by, Simon of Cyrene, who was coming in from the country, the father of Alexander and Rufus, to carry his cross. And they brought him to a place called Golgotha (which means the place of a skull). And they offered him wine mingled with myrrh; but he did not take it. And they crucified him, and divided his garments among them, casting lots for them, to decide what each should take. And it was the third hour, when they crucified him. And the inscription of the charge against him read, 'The King of the Jews'. And with him they crucified two robbers, one on his right and one on his left. And those who passed by derided him, wagging their heads, and saying, 'Aha! You who would destroy the temple, and build it in three days, save yourself, and come down from the cross!' So also the chief priests mocked him to one another with the scribes, saying, 'He saved others; he cannot save himself. Let the Christ, the King of Israel, come down from the cross, that we may see and believe.' Those who were crucified with him also reviled him.*

Mt 27:32–44
*As they went out, they came upon a man of Cyrene, Simon by name; this man they compelled to carry his cross. And when they came to a place called Golgotha (which means the place of a skull), they offered him wine to drink, mingled with gall; but when he tasted it, he could not drink it. And when they had crucified him, they divided his garments among them by casting lots; then they sat down and kept watch over him there. And over his head they put the charge against him: 'This is Jesus the King of the Jews.' Then two robbers were crucified with him, one on the right and one on the left. And those who passed by derided him, wagging their heads, and saying, 'You who would destroy the temple, and build it in three days, save yourself! If you are the Son of God, come down from the cross.' So also the chief priests, with the scribes and elders, mocked him, saying, 'He saved others; he cannot save himself. He is the King of Israel; let him come down from the cross, and we will believe in him. He trusts in God; let God deliver him now, if he desires him; for he said, "I am the Son of God."' And the robbers who were crucified with him also reviled him in the same way.*

Lk 23:23–49
*And as they led him away, they seized one Simon of Cyrene, who was coming in from the country, and laid on him his cross, to carry it behind Jesus. And there followed him a great multitude of people, and of women who bewailed and lamented him. But Jesus turning to them said, 'Daughters of Jerusalem, do not weep for me, but weep for yourselves and for your children. For behold, the days are coming when they will say, "Blessed are the barren, and the wombs that never bore, and the breasts that never gave suck!" Then*

they will begin to say to the mountains, "Fall on us"; and to the hills, "Cover us." For if they do this when the wood is green, what will happen when it is dry?' Two others also, who were criminals, were led away to be put to death with him. And when they came to the place which is called the skull, there they crucified him, and the criminals, one on the right and one on the left. And Jesus said, 'Father, forgive them; for they know not what they do.' And they cast lots to divide his garments. And the people stood by, watching; but the rulers scoffed at him saying, 'He saved others; let him save himself, if he is the Christ of God, his Chosen One!' The soldiers also mocked him, coming up and offering him vinegar, and saying, 'If you are the King of the Jews, save yourself!' There was also an inscription over him, 'This is the King of the Jews.' One of the criminals who were hanged railed at him, saying, 'Are you not the Christ? Save yourself and us!' But the other rebuked him, saying, 'Do you not fear God, since you are under the same sentence of condemnation? And we indeed justly; for we are receiving the due reward of our deeds; but this man has done nothing wrong.' And he said, 'Jesus, remember me when you come into your kingdom.' And he said to him, 'Truly, I say to you, today you will be with me in Paradise.'

Jn 19: 17–27
So they took Jesus, and he went out, bearing his own cross, to the place called the place of a skull, which is called in Hebrew Golgotha. There they crucified him, and with him two others, one on either side, and Jesus between them. Pilate also wrote a title and put it on the cross; it read, 'Jesus of Nazareth, the King of the Jews.' Many of the Jews read this title, for the place where Jesus was crucified was near the city; and it was written in Hebrew, in Latin, and in Greek. The chief priests of the Jews then said to Pilate, 'Do not write, "The King of the Jews", but, "This man said, I am the King of the Jews."' Pilate answered, 'What I have written,

*I have written.' When the soldiers had crucified Jesus they took his garments and made four parts, one for each soldier; also his tunic. But the tunic was without seam, woven from top to bottom; so they said to one another, 'Let us not tear it, but cast lots for it to see whose it shall be.' This was to fulfil the Scripture, 'They parted my garments among them, and for my clothing they cast lots.' So the soldiers did this. But standing by the cross of Jesus were his mother, and his mother's sister, Mary the wife of Clopas, and Mary Magdalene. When Jesus saw his mother, and the disciple whom he loved standing near, he said to his mother, 'Woman, behold your son!' Then he said to the disciple, 'Behold your mother!' And from that hour the disciple took her to his own home.*

Only one incident is recorded by all the Synoptic Gospels concerning Jesus' journey from the residence of Pilate to Calvary; the forced recruitment by the soldiers of a passer-by, Simon from Cyrene, to help Jesus to carry the cross. He has never been heard of before nor is he mentioned again. The help that Simon gave to Jesus is commemorated at one of the Stations of the Cross. Several additional incidents are listed at the Stations of the Cross: the three falls of Jesus under the weight of the gibbet, his meeting with Mary, his mother, and with Veronica on whose scarf the image of Jesus is believed to have imprinted itself, but these purported happenings are all without New Testament foundation. The encounter of Jesus with the lamenting women of Jerusalem is mentioned in the Gospel of Luke, but there alone (Lk 23:27–31).

The Synoptic evangelists report that Jesus was crucified at the third hour of the day, i.e. nine o'clock in the morning, together with two other condemned Jews on a hill called 'the skull', or Golgotha in Aramaic. According to John, the crucifixion happened three hours later, at midday, the sixth hour. (The Jewish night ran from 6 p.m. to 6 a.m., and the day from 6 a.m. to 6 p.m.) The reference to a drink of wine mixed with myrrh or vinegar (Mk 15:23; Mt 27:34; Jn 19:29) is more likely to stem from the evangelists' wish to see another fulfilment of Scripture (Ps 69:21) than from the hardened Roman executioners' sympathy for a crucified Jew. It is true that in Mark 15:36 and Matthew 27:48 some Jews offer Jesus a drink, but they give him vinegar in straight fulfilment of the words of the Psalm. Their purpose was not to diminish consciousness, as some kind-hearted later rabbis proposed that one should assist people to be executed (Babylonian Talmud Sanhedrin 43a), but to prolong the life of the crucified out of curiosity: they wanted to see whether Elijah would come to the rescue of the dying Jesus.

Jesus' cross bore an inscription or title (*titulus*), composed by Pilate himself if we believe John, giving the reason for his execution. Not one of the four Gospels fully agrees with any other in recording the short text. The briefest is Mark's with 'The King of the Jews', and the longest is the version of the Fourth Gospel, 'Jesus of Nazareth, the King of the Jews', with John's added note that the inscription was in Hebrew (Aramaic), Latin and Greek (Jn 19:19–20). John further remarks that the Jewish chief priests tried to quibble and petitioned Pilate to correct the text to read: 'This man said, I am King of the Jews.' However, they were given short shrift by the governor: 'What I have written, I have written' – *Ho gegrapha, gegrapha* – *Quod scripsi, scripsi* (Jn 19:21–2). With this, the Jewish delegation disappears from John's story. No doubt they rushed to the Temple to perform their other duties. Contrary to the Synoptics, the author of the Fourth Gospel does not bring the chief priests to the cross.

The evangelists find not a single Jew to say a kind word about Jesus. Not only the chief priests, the scribes and the elders, who pursued him to Calvary, but also all the passers-by, and even the two other crucified criminals, according to Mark and Matthew, mocked and railed him. In Luke only one of them did so, while the other begged for the intercession of Jesus and received from him a promise of reassurance: 'Today you will be with me in Paradise' (Lk 23:39–43).

The compassionate Luke, endeavouring to improve Mark's version, introduces elements of pity which are no doubt of his own creation. Note among his retouches, in addition to the repentant robber, Jesus' healing of the wounded slave of the high priest in Gethsemane (Lk 22:51), the lament of the sympathetic women of Jerusalem (Lk 23:27), the multitude of onlookers beating their breasts after the death of Jesus, and the mention of *all* his acquaintances standing at some distance from the cross (Lk 48–9).

In the crucifixion story itself Luke departs from Mark on an important point. He introduces a saying of the dying Jesus immediately after the mention, 'there they crucified him'. His words run: 'Father, forgive them; for they know not what they do' (Lk 23:34). Attentive readers are bound to be puzzled by the absence of this verse, so typical of the thought of Jesus, from half of the ancient codices of Luke and from all the other Gospels. Has Jesus' prayer of forgiveness been deliberately deleted? Also, for whom does Jesus beg God's pardon? The context suggests that the pronoun 'they' most probably points the Roman soldiers, the executioners who attached him to the cross: 'there *they* crucified him'. The same Roman soldiers remain the subjects of the next sentence: 'and *they* cast lots' (Lk 23:34). But according to the main New Testament tradition the Romans were not the real guilty party in the story of the Passion. They had already been exonerated when Pilate was whitewashed; so Jesus did not need to pray for them to be forgiven. The remaining alternative is that 'they' refers to the Jews. Attributing their action against Jesus to ignorance, 'they know not what they do', would be in harmony with the thought of the primitive Jerusalem church. The Jewish leaders acted in ignorance, the author of the Acts of the Apostles makes Peter say (Acts 3:17). But reference to mitigating circumstances in favour of the Jews would not tally with the story-line adopted by Mark, and especially by Matthew with his cry, 'His blood be on us and on our children' (Mt 27:25). Hence the editors of the first two Gospels ignored the saying, 'Father, forgive them', and in the course of time many copyists even excised the verse from the manuscripts of the gentle Luke, thus revealing the basic anti-Jewish tendency of early Christianity.

## 12. The death of Jesus

Mk 15:33–41

*And when the sixth hour had come, there was darkness over the whole land until the ninth hour. And at the ninth hour Jesus cried with a loud voice, 'Eloi, Eloi lama sabachthani?' which means, 'My God, my God, why hast thou forsaken me?' And some of the bystanders hearing it said, 'Behold, he is calling Elijah.' And one ran and, filling a sponge full of vinegar, put it on a reed and gave it to him to drink, saying, 'Wait, let us see whether Elijah will come and take him down.' And Jesus uttered a loud cry, and breathed his last. And the curtain of the temple was torn in two, from top to bottom. And when the centurion, who stood facing him, saw that he thus breathed his last, he said, 'Truly this man is a son of God!' There were also women looking on from afar, among whom were Mary Magdalene and Mary mother of James the younger and Joses, and Salome, who, when he was in Galilee, followed him, and ministered to him; and also many other women who came up with him to Jerusalem.*

Mt 27:46–56
*Now from the sixth hour there was darkness over the whole land until the ninth hour. And about the ninth hour Jesus cried with a loud voice, 'Eli, Eli, lama sabachthani?', that is, 'My God, my God, why hast thou forsaken me?' And some of the bystanders hearing it said, 'This man is calling Elijah.' And one of them at once ran and took a sponge, filled it with vinegar, and put it on a reed, and gave it to him to drink. But the others said, 'Wait, let us see whether Elijah will come to save him.' And Jesus cried again with a loud voice and yielded up his spirit. And behold the curtain of the temple was torn in two, from top to bottom; and the earth shook and the rocks were split; the tombs were also opened, and many bodies of the saints who had fallen asleep were raised, and coming out of the tombs after his resurrection they went into the holy city and appeared to many. When the centurion and those who were with him, keeping watch over Jesus, saw the earthquake and what took place, they were filled with awe, and said, 'Truly this was a son of God!' There were also many women there, looking on from afar, who had followed Jesus from Galilee, ministering to him; among them were Mary Magdalene, and Mary the mother of James and Joseph, and the mother of the sons of Zebedee.*

Lk 23:44–9
*It was now about the sixth hour, and there was darkness over the whole land until the ninth hour, while the sun's light failed; and the curtain of the temple was torn in two. Then Jesus, crying with*

*a loud voice, said, 'Father, into thy hands I commit my spirit!' And having said this he breathed his last. Now when the centurion saw what had taken place, he praised God, and said, 'Certainly this man was innocent!' And all the multitudes who assembled to see the sight, when they saw what had taken place, returned home beating their breasts. And all his acquaintances and the women who had followed him from Galilee stood at a distance and saw these things.*

Jn 19:28–37
*After this Jesus, knowing that all was now finished, said (to fulfil the Scripture), 'I thirst.' A bowl full of vinegar stood there; so they put a sponge full of the vinegar on hyssop and held it to his mouth. When Jesus had received the vinegar, he said, 'It is finished'; and he bowed his head and gave up his spirit. Since it was the Day of Preparation, in order to prevent the bodies from remaining on the cross on the Sabbath (for that Sabbath was a high day), the Jews asked Pilate that their legs might be broken, and that they might be taken away. So the soldiers came and broke the legs of the first, and of the other who had been crucified with him, and when they came to Jesus and saw that he was already dead, they did not break his legs. But one of the soldiers pierced his side with a spear, and at once there came out blood and water. . . . For these things took place that the Scripture might be fulfilled, 'Not a bone of him shall be broken.' And again another Scripture says, 'They shall look on him whom they have pierced.'*

The end of Jesus, Mark and Matthew tell their readers, came soon at the ninth hour (three o'clock in the afternoon) after six hours of agony on the cross. In John the time between crucifixion and death is reduced to three hours, from noon till 3 p.m. The first two evangelists record a cry of Jesus, *Eloi, Eloi, lama sabachthani?* (My God, my

God, why hast thou forsaken me?). The words are the Aramaic equivalent of the opening line of the Hebrew Psalm 22 (*Eli, Eli, lama 'azabtani*), and since two other verses of the same Psalm are cited in the crucifixion narrative, one apropos of the railing of Jesus by the passers-by and the other about the division of his clothes with the help of a die (Ps 22:8, 19), the quotations are thought by many to constitute a literary and theological device employed by Mark and Matthew. The events are presented as the fulfilment of Scripture. However, it must be observed that the words attributed to Jesus, *Eloi, Eloi, lama sabachthani?*, are given in Mark in Aramaic and not in the original Hebrew, the language in which the Psalms were normally recited by most Jews in the Temple and the synagogue. I think the best explanation for this unexpected use is that the phrase had become in the vernacular of the time of Jesus a kind of proverbial saying, expressing religious incomprehension and bewilderment. It is fascinating to note that Mark and Matthew claim that the bystanders misheard and misunderstood the cry. They believed that Jesus was calling, not on God, but on the miracle-working prophet Elijah, and excitedly commented: 'Wait. Let us see whether Elijah will come to take him down' (Mk 15:36; Mt 27:49).

John emphasizes that Jesus had truly expired; hence there was no need to break his legs, as was done to the two other crucified to precipitate the end before the start of the Sabbath and of Passover. However, just to make sure, one of the soldiers pierced Jesus' side with a spear and was satisfied that he was no longer alive (Jn 19:31–7).

Mark and Matthew refer also to another scream without recording the words. Luke's tradition identifies it as a peaceful parting prayer: 'Father, into thy hands I commit my spirit!' With this last cry Jesus gave up the ghost (Mk 15:33–7; Mt 27:45–50; Lk 23:44–6).

According to the Synoptic Gospels, Jesus died abandoned by his family and his male friends. The only sympathetic witnesses of his last moments were a few women who faithfully followed him from Galilee to Jerusalem. Frightened of approaching the crucified, they watched him die from afar. Those named are Mary Magdalene, Mary mother of James and Joses, and Salome, the wife of Zebedee and mother of the apostles James and John (Mk 15:40–41; Mt 27:55–6). Among the absentees figure all the apostles and disciples, and Mary, mother of Jesus and the rest of his family. Luke is vague, but slightly more generous; he brings to the proximity of the cross all the acquaintances of Jesus and the women who had followed him from Galilee (Lk 23:49).

In the Fourth Gospel there are no jeering spectators, no chief priests or passers-by. The small group of sympathizers who stood at the foot of the cross is not quite the same as in the Synoptics. The ever-faithful Mary Magdalene is there, as is also the other Mary, here identified as the wife of Clopas. But the chief difference consists in the presence of the mother of Jesus and the apostle whom he especially loved (identified as John son of Zebedee by Christian tradition). John records that Jesus entrusted his mother and his favourite disciple to each other's care. 'It is finished', or perhaps better 'It [the whole prophetic destiny of Christ] is fulfilled' constitutes Jesus' last theological statement in the Fourth Gospel (Jn 19:23–30).

The three Synoptic Gospels describe various miraculous events preceding and following the death of Jesus. They allude to sudden darkness at noon lasting until 3 p.m., a common element of apocalyptic imagery (Mk 25:33; Mt 27:45;

Lk 23:44). They also mention the rending of the curtain of the Temple (Mk 15:38; Mt 27:51; Lk 23:45), an event in which Christianity has seen the symbolical end of Judaism. Matthew speaks also of an earthquake, another apocalyptic feature, which opened tombs and allowed many bodies contained in them to rise from the dead (Mt 27:52–3).

All three Synoptic Gospels record the proclamation of the centurion, head of the execution squad, that Jesus was a son of God (Mark and Matthew) or an innocent man (Luke). The privilege of being the first to confess the greatness of Jesus after his death is granted by Mark to a Gentile and, perhaps most significantly, to a Roman.

## 13. The burial of Jesus

Mk 15:42–7
*And when evening had come, since it was the Day of Preparation, that is, the day before the Sabbath, Joseph of Arimathea, a respected member of the council, who was also himself looking for the kingdom of God, took courage and went to Pilate, and asked for the body of Jesus. And Pilate wondered if he were already dead; and summoning the centurion, he asked him whether he was already dead. And when he learned from the centurion that he was dead, he granted the body to Joseph. And he bought a linen shroud, and taking him down, wrapped him in the linen shroud, and laid him in a tomb which had been hewn out of the rock; and he rolled a stone against the door of the tomb. Mary Magdalene and Mary the mother of Joses saw where he was laid.*

Mt 27:57–66
*When it was evening, there came a rich man from Arimathea, named Joseph, who also was a disciple of Jesus. He went to Pilate*

*and asked for the body of Jesus. Then Pilate ordered it to be given to him. And Joseph took the body, and wrapped it in a clean linen shroud, and laid it in his own new tomb, which he had hewn in the rock; and he rolled a great stone to the door of the tomb, and departed. Mary Magdalene and the other Mary were there, sitting opposite the sepulchre. Next day, that is, after the Day of Preparation, the chief priests and the Pharisees gathered before Pilate and said, 'Sir, we remember how that impostor said, while he was still alive, "After three days I will rise again." Therefore order the sepulchre to be made secure until the third day, lest his disciples go and steal him away, and tell the people, "He has risen from the dead," and the last fraud will be worse than the first.' Pilate said to them, 'You have a guard of soldiers; go, make it as secure as you can.' So they went and made the sepulchre secure by sealing the stone and setting a guard.*

Lk 23:50–56

*Now there was a man named Joseph of the Jewish town of Arimathea. He was a member of the council, a good and righteous man, who had not consented to their purpose and deed, and he was looking for the kingdom of God. This man went to Pilate and asked for the body of Jesus. Then he took it down and wrapped it in a linen shroud, and laid it in a rock-hewn tomb, where no one had ever yet been laid. It was the Day of Preparation, and the Sabbath was beginning. The women who had come with him from Galilee followed, and saw the tomb, and how his body was laid; then they returned, and prepared spices and ointments. On the Sabbath they rested according to the commandment.*

Jn 19:38–42

*After this Joseph of Arimathea, who was a disciple of Jesus, but secretly, for fear of the Jews, asked Pilate that he might take away the body of Jesus, and Pilate gave him leave. So he came and took away his body. Nicodemus also, who had at first come to him by night, came bringing a mixture of myrrh and aloes, about a hundred pounds' weight. They took the body of Jesus, and bound it in linen cloths with the spices, as is the burial custom of the Jews. Now in the place where he was crucified, there was a garden, and in the garden a new tomb, where no one had ever been laid. So because of the Jewish Day of Preparation, as the tomb was close at hand, they laid Jesus there.*

The three Synoptic evangelists report that at the approach of nightfall on Friday, shortly before Sabbath began, Joseph of Arimathea, a member of the Sanhedrin and a crypto-sympathizer, obtained permission from Pilate to take down the body from the cross. Luke specifies that Joseph had disagreed with his fellow councillors regarding Jesus, but no one mentions this in the context of the trial of Jesus by the Sanhedrin. The centurion in command of the executioners testified before the governor that Jesus had already died, and Joseph was granted permission to proceed with a hasty burial. Without the use of the customary spices, he wrapped the body in a linen shroud which he had purchased. He then laid the body in a freshly hewn rock tomb, the entrance of which was protected from wild animals and thieves by a large and heavy rolling stone. The Jewish custom was to leave the body in the tomb cave until the flesh disintegrated. At some later date the bones were collected and placed into a box made of wood, plaster or stone. These boxes or ossuaries were then kept in family burial tombs. In the Synoptics Mary Magdalene and another woman, also named Mary (so Mark and Matthew) or Galilean women (Luke), are said to have watched Joseph of Arimathea at the tomb (Mk 15:42–7; Mt 27:57–61; Lk 23:50–56).

The tradition transmitted by John is in partial agreement with the Synoptics. Joseph of Arimathea, a clandestine follower of Jesus 'for fear of the Jews', is the protagonist, but in John he is joined by a second secret disciple, Nicodemus (Jn 3:2). Joseph does not buy the linen shroud; it is brought along by Nicodemus together with a mixture of spices weighing about 100 pounds. (How he put his hands on all this at a moment's notice and carried it outside the city remains unexplained.) Be this as it may, as the start of Passover was close, the two Jewish dignitaries hurriedly buried Jesus in a new tomb in a nearby garden without being observed by any female witness (Jn 19:38–42).

Matthew further notes, no doubt with the hindsight of later Christian polemical considerations, that the Jewish leaders, fearful that the disciples of Jesus might steal his body and stage a fake fulfilment of his predicted resurrection from the dead, asked Pilate to keep the tomb under military observation. 'Do it yourselves' seems to have been the governor's sharp reply. So the chief priests sealed the entrance of the cave and sentries were posted there to keep away intruders.

The account of the burial of Jesus closes the Gospel story of the Passion. As has been made obvious in the running commentary, the evangelists are not altogether logical in themselves, nor is the tradition underlying the Synoptic Gospels compatible with that of the Fourth Gospel. Our next task therefore is to state the problems as clearly as possible both in their New Testament dimension and in comparison with all the relevant data arising from Jewish and Roman history and culture of the age of Jesus.

# III

## The Passion accounts compared with one another and with sources from outside the New Testament

Having completed the survey of the Passion story in the separate Gospels, the moment has arrived for the detective-historian to cast a comprehensive glance at the evidence and investigate how the accounts of the four evangelists relate to one another. A list of the main common features appearing in the Gospels followed by another consisting of the obvious differences will facilitate the overall comparison.

There is general *agreement* among the evangelists on seven incidents of the Passion story.

1. They all place the arrest of Jesus in a garden outside Jerusalem late in the evening, after supper. John expressly mentions that the soldiers sent to look for Jesus were carrying lanterns and torches (Jn 18:3).

2. The following morning Jesus was transferred from the palace of the high priest (Caiaphas) to the residence of the Roman governor to be tried by Pontius Pilate on a political charge.

3. During the hearing the question of the Passover amnesty was brought up by Pilate.

4. Pilate condemned Jesus to death and an inscription affixed to the cross stated that Jesus was crucified as 'The King of the Jews'.

5. Jesus' garments were divided among the members of the execution squad, four Roman soldiers according to John (Jn 19:23).

6. Jesus died on the cross.

7. He was immediately buried in a rock tomb, the entrance of which was closed by a large rolling stone.

The five *disagreements* neatly fall between the Synoptic Gospels and John.

1. The date of the Last Supper, arrest and cruxifixion of Jesus: Thursday evening/Friday, 15 Nisan = Passover (Synoptics); *or* Thursday evening/Friday, 14 Nisan = *eve* of Passover (John). In John 15 Nisan = Passover falls on Friday evening/Saturday (Jn 19:14, 31).

2. The reason why the apostles left Jesus: they fled (Synoptics) *or* were allowed to go (John).

3. The venue and character of the proceedings during the night following the arrest: Jesus was taken to Caiaphas and tried and sentenced on the religious charge of blasphemy (Mark and Matthew with a revised scenario in Luke) *or* he was first interrogated by the former high priest Annas and then sent to Caiaphas without religious trial or sentence (John). The issue of the competence of a Jewish court to execute a capital sentence (John) is also relevant here.

4. The identity of the persons at the cross: Galilean women (Synoptics) *or* the mother of Jesus and his beloved disciple as well as Galilean women (John).

5. The identity of the men who buried Jesus: Joseph of Arimathea (Synoptics) *or* Joseph of Arimathea and Nicodemus (John).

Nothing is more revealing in the comparative study of texts than a parallel presentation of agreements and disagreements. Therefore in order to assist the reader to perceive at a simple glance identities and discrepancies among the Gospels, the contents of the Passion narratives are printed in four parallel columns. Mark's Gospel, being the ultimate source of the Jesus story in the Synoptics, appears in the first column and thus serves as pattern. Peculiarities in the diverse Gospels are set in bold print; identical reports are marked by –"–, and missing items by [----].

| MARK | | MATTHEW | |
|---|---|---|---|
| *Last Supper* (Eucharist) | 14:22–5 | *Last Supper* (–"–) | 26:26–9 |
| [Passover meal 14:12] | | [–"–26:17] | |

| MARK | | MATTHEW | |
|---|---|---|---|
| *Arrest* | 14:26, 43–52 | *Arrest* | 26:30, 47–56 |
| Judas + chief priest's men | | –"– | |
| Arrest | | –"– | |
| Disciple draws sword [----] | | –"–Jesus stops disciple | |
| Jesus protests innocence | | –"– | |
| Disciples flee | | –"– | |

| MARK | | MATTHEW | |
|---|---|---|---|
| *Jesus in the high priest's house* | 14:53–65 | *Jesus in Caiaphas' house* | 26:57–68 |
| Night trial by Sanhedrin | | –"– | |
| Witnesses rejected by court | | –"– | |
| High priest: Are you Christ? | | –"– | |
| Jesus: **Yes.** Seated on right of God | | You say so | |
| High priest: Blasphemy – death | | –"– | |
| Assault on Jesus by judges and guards | | –"– | |
| | | [----] | |

| LUKE | | JOHN | |
|---|---|---|---|
| *Last Supper* (–"–) | 22:15–20 | *Last Supper* [**No Euch.**] | 13:1–2, 29 |
| [–"–22:7–8, *15*] | | **Before** Passover | |
| | | **Judas to buy things for Passover** | |
| | | | |
| *Arrest* | 22:39, 47–53 | *Arrest* | 18:2–11 |
| –"– | | Judas+**cohort of soldiers** | |
| –"– | | From chief priests. **Fall to ground** | |
| | | **Jesus: Let disciples go** | |
| –"–Jesus stops disciple, **heals** slave | | **Peter** resists. Jesus stops him | |
| [----] | | [----] | |
| | | | |
| *Jesus in high priest's house* | 22:54 | *Jesus in **Annas'** house* | 18:12–14 |
| | | [**No Jewish trial**] | |
| [**No night trial**] | | **Cohort+tribune+Jewish officers** | |
| [----] | | Jesus **interrogated** by **Annas** | |
| [----] | | **Jesus claims innocence** | |
| [----] | | **Annas sends him to Pilate** | |
| [----] | | | |
| [----] | | | |
| **Mockery by guard** | 22:63–5 | | |

| MARK | | MATTHEW | |
|---|---|---|---|
| *Morning meeting* | 15:1 | *Morning meeting* | 27:1–2 |
| Case sent to Pilate | | –"– | |
| | | *Judas' suicide* | 27:3–10 |

| | | | |
|---|---|---|---|
| *Jesus before Pilate* | 15:2–5 | *Jesus before Pilate* | 27:11–14 |
| Pilate: Are you King of Jews? | | –"– | |
| Jesus: You say so | | –"– | |
| Accused by chief priests | | –"– | |
| No answer by Jesus | | –"– | |
| Pilate astonished | | –"– **greatly** | |

*Morning council*          22:66–71
**Judges: Are you Christ?**
**You say so.–"–**
**Are you Son of God?**
**Judges: We heard him**
**[No sentence]**

---

*Jesus before Pilate*          23:2–5

**Chief priests charge Jesus**
**–"–**
**–"–**
**–"–**
**–"–**
**–"–**
**Pilate: I find no crime**
**Chief priests: Troublemaker**
  **from Galilee to Jerusalem**

*Jesus before Pilate*          18:28–38
**Early on eve of Passover**
**Pilate: What is the charge?**
**Pilate: You judge him**
**Jews: We cannot execute**
**Pilate: Are you King of Jews?**
**Jesus: Kingdom not of the**
  **world**
**–"–**

---

*Jesus before Herod*          23:6–12
**Jesus questioned, mocked,**
  **returned to Pilate**
Pilate: **No guilt.**
Pilate: **Will flog and release**
  **Jesus?**

| MARK | | MATTHEW | |
|---|---|---|---|
| *Passover amnesty* | 15:6–14 | *Passover amnesty* | 27:15–25 |
| Pilate: Release King of Jews? | | Pilate: **Barabbas or Jesus?** | |
| | | **Pilate's wife's nightmare** | |
| Chief priests urge for Barabbas | | –"– | |
| Pilate: What to do with Jesus? | | –"– | |
| Chief priests: Crucify him! | | –"– | |
| | | **Pilate washes hands** | |
| | | **Jews: His blood be on us** | |

| MARK | | MATTHEW | |
|---|---|---|---|
| *Sentence of death* | 15:15–20 | *Sentence of death* | 27:26–31 |
| Barabbas released | | –"– | |
| Jesus flogged | | –"– | |
| Delivered to be crucified | | –"– | |
| Mocked by soldiers | | –"– | |

| LUKE | | JOHN | |
|---|---|---|---|

| | | | |
|---|---|---|---|
| *Passover amnesty* | 23:17–23 | *Passover amnesty* | 19:38–40 |
| **Jews: Crucify Jesus, free Barabbas** | | | |
| _"_ | | _"_ | |
| _"_ | | _"_ | |
| _"_ | | _"_ | |

| | | | |
|---|---|---|---|
| *Sentence of death* | 23:24–5 | *Sentence of death* | 19:1–15 |
| _"_ | | [----] | |
| [----] | | _"_ | |
| _"_ | | Mocked by soldiers | |
| [----] | | **Pilate: No crime** | |
| | | **Behold the man** | |
| | | **Pilate: You crucify him** | |
| | | **Jews: Son of God** | |
| | | **Jesus: Jews more guilty** | |
| | | **Pilate: Will release him** | |
| | | **Chief priests: No friend of Caesar** | |
| | | **Jesus delivered to them** | |

| *Crucifixion* | 15:21–32 | *Crucifixion* | 27:32–44 |
|---|---|---|---|
| Simon of Cyrene | | –"– | |
| **His sons** | | [----] | |
| Golgotha | | –"– | |
| Wine+myrrh | | –"– | |
| Crucifixion+2 | | –"– | |
| Garments | | –"– | |
| Inscription | | –"– | |
| Passers-by | | –"– | |
| Chief priests | | –"– | |
| Robbers | | –"– | |

| *Death* | 15:33–41 | *Death* | 27:45–56 |
|---|---|---|---|
| Darkness from 6 to 9 | | –"– | |
| Eloi | | Eli | |
| Calling Elijah | | –"– | |
| Sponge | | –"– | |
| Last cry | | –"– | |
| Curtain split | | –"–+**tombs–saints** | |
| Centurion: son of God | | –"– | |
| Women: M. Magdalene, Mary, Salome | | –"– Wife of Zebedee | |

| LUKE | | JOHN | |
|---|---|---|---|
| *Crucifixion* | 23:26–43 | *Crucifixion* | 19:16–27 |
| –"– | | [----] | |
| [----] | | [----] | |
| **Multitude+Jerusalem women** | | Golgotha | |
| Crucifixion+2 | | –"– | |
| **Father, forgive** | | Crucifixion+2 | |
| Garments | | Inscription **by Pilate** | |
| Rulers (chief priests) | | **Chief priests quibble** | |
| **Mocked by soldiers** | | Garments | |
| Inscription | | **At cross mother of Jesus+** | |
| Robber reviling | | **Disciple+two Marys** | |
| **One robber praying** | | | |
| **Promise by Jesus** | | | |

| LUKE | | JOHN | |
|---|---|---|---|
| *Death* | 23:44–9 | *Death* | 19:28–37 |
| –"–+ curtain split | | [----] | |
| [----] | | [----] | |
| [----] | | [----] | |
| [----] | | **I thirst+** wine | |
| **Father, into thy hands** | | **It is finished** | |
| | | [----] | |
| Centurion | | [----] | |
| **Repentant multitude** | | **Legs broken** | |
| **All acquaintances+**women | | **Side pierced** | |

| MARK | | MATTHEW | |
|---|---|---|---|
| *Burial* | 15:42–7 | *Burial* | 27:57–61 |
| Joseph of Arimathea – Pilate | | –"– | |
| Member of council | | **Rich man** | |
| **Centurion reporting** | | [----] | |
| Body wrapped in shroud | | –"– | |
| Rock tomb+stone | | –"– | |
| M. Magdalene+Mary | | –"– | |
| | | **Guard posted** | |

| LUKE | | JOHN | |
|---|---|---|---|
| *Burial* | 23:50–56 | *Burial* | 19:38–42 |
| _"_ | | _"_ | |
| _"_ | | Disciple | |
| [----] | | [----] | |
| _"_ | | **Nicodemus+spices** | |
| _"_ | | _"_ | |
| | | Tomb **in garden** | |
| | | [----] | |

# I. Comments on the general agreements

Most of the agreements require no further comment, nevertheless four issues deriving from them may benefit from some additional explanation.

1. Although this is not explicitly formulated, it would seem that substantial disparity is concealed in the terminological variations attested in John and the Synoptics concerning the composition of the party which arrested Jesus in the garden of Gethsemane. In the Synoptics the priestly authorities dispatch armed men led by 'the officers of the Jews'. They appear to represent the Jewish Temple police. John, by contrast, refers to members of what seems to be a military unit, *speira* in Greek, under the command of a high-ranking *chiliarchos* (major or colonel). These soldiers were accompanied by 'the officers of the Jews' (Jn 18:12). A *speira* corresponds to the Roman cohort, and its commander is a *tribunus* or tribune, the Latin equivalent of the Greek *chiliarchos*. The words occur elsewhere in the military vocabulary of the New Testament. The Roman centurion Cornelius, who was to become a Christian, belonged to the 'Italian cohort' stationed in Caesarea, and Paul was arrested in the Temple by the Roman tribune Claudius Lysias (Acts 10:1; 21:31; 23:26). Does this suggest that Jesus was apprehended by a unit of *Roman* soldiers assisted by Jewish liaison officers and not by Jewish Temple policemen? This would put a different complexion on the whole Passion story.

The theory that Jesus was taken into custody by Roman legionaries has been advanced among others by Paul Winter (*On the Trial of Jesus*, 1974, pp. 61–9), Fergus Millar ('Reflections on the Trials of Jesus', in *A Tribute to Geza*

*Vermes*, 1990, p. 370) and Paula Fredriksen ( *Jesus of Nazareth, the King of the Jews*, 1999, p. 258). The interpretation of the military vocabulary as alluding to the Roman army has, however, been challenged in the light of Josephus' use of the same expressions in a Jewish context ( *Jewish Antiquities* 17:215; *Jewish War* 2:578). Nevertheless Josephus definitely alludes to armies, either to those of the Herodian ruler Archelaus or to the revolutionary forces of John of Gischala during the first war against Rome. These forces were explicitly organized on the model of the Roman legions. It is however debatable whether the nomenclature appropriate for an army can simply be transferred to the Temple police.

2. The next query regards the Passover amnesty. As has been noted, such an amnesty is nowhere mentioned outside the Gospels, not even in Josephus, who was so well informed about first-century AD matters, and the evangelists themselves fail to agree on its precise nature. Was it a Roman practice (Lk 23:17) or a Jewish usage (Jn 18:39), or was the person to benefit from the free pardon chosen by the governor or by the people (though the latter alternative is intrinsically unlikely)? Hence the historicity of the amnesty is questionable. On the other hand, the imminently expected announcement of the release of a prisoner could account for the foregathering at the palace of Pilate of a multitude of Jews (Mk 16:6–11; Mt 27:15–18; Lk 23:4).

3. The division of the garments of Jesus among the legionaries is conceivable, though it may be asked whether the soldiers would be interested in the scourged Jesus' bloodstained clothes. On the other hand, the account may be due to the evangelists' wish to draw attention to another fulfilment of Scripture: 'They divide my garments among them, and for my raiment they cast lots' (Ps 22:18).

4. That Jesus actually died on the cross is firmly stated in every Gospel. The emphasis, especially in John, is probably meant to refute in advance doubts about the reality of the resurrection: the disappearance of the body of Jesus was not due to the revival of a comatose man. The recovery of crucified men was not unheard of. After Josephus' intercession, three of his crucified Jewish friends were taken down from the cross on Titus' order and were looked after by physicians, with the consequent return to health of one of the three (*Life* 420). The Islamic teaching that the death of Jesus on the cross was merely apparent may have derived from such early rumours.

## 2. Comments on disagreements between the Synoptics and John

Some of the discrepancies in the story of the Passion between the Synoptics and John present the interpreter with serious dilemmas. The ultimate question is: Are these contradictions reconcilable or must one choose one of the alternatives and reject the other?

1. Chronology stands at the top of the list of disagreements. The time difference between John and the Synoptics is admittedly only twenty-four hours, but the possible repercussions are enormous.

The Last Supper in the Synoptic Gospels is a Passover meal. This is clearly indicated in the run-up to the event, with disciples dispatched to make the necessary preparations for the Passover dinner that same evening. It is also expressly declared by Jesus in Luke: 'I have earnestly desired to eat this Passover with you' (Lk 22:15). Yet if the Passover supper was eaten on the prescribed date and at the prescribed time, i.e. around 6 p.m. at the start of 15 Nisan, the further stages of the Passion story are affected by major consequential problems: events that are not supposed to happen during a feast day (e.g. the trial of a capital case) are said to have occurred on this occasion. By contrast, if the chronology of the Fourth Gospel is followed – i.e. the meal eaten on 14 Nisan was not a Passover meal – there would be no legal difficulties, but the link of the Last Supper with the Passover dinner would disappear. Yet these paschal roots of the Eucharist are taken for granted not only by the Synoptics, but also by St Paul writing fifteen to forty-five years before them. Paul states that the Lord's supper was celebrated on the night of his betrayal (1 Cor 11:23) shortly before his immolation as 'our Passover lamb' (1 Cor 5:7).

It is possible to circumnavigate these danger points by surmising that Jesus' religious calendar differed from that of mainstream Judaism. This hypothesis has been advanced in the wake of the discovery of the sectarian calendar of the Dead Sea Scrolls. The Qumran-Essene year of 364 days is so arranged that the first day of the first month (Nisan) always falls on a Wednesday, and so too does Passover two weeks later on 15 Nisan. If Jesus had embraced the Essene time reckoning, he could have had his Passover dinner on an earlier evening than the Temple priests and their coreligionists. In fact, however, this theory creates more difficulties than it resolves. In the first instance, there is no valid evidence in the Scrolls of any influence of sectarian (Essene) religious practice on the Galilean Jesus. Moreover, if Jesus ate his Passover meal on Tuesday evening, as the Essenes would have done, and was tried and executed the following day, we are left with the insoluble riddle stemming from the repeated assertion in the

Gospels that the day following the crucifixion was a Sabbath. The Qumran-inspired solution is therefore a red herring.

2. The next difference is connected with the flight of the disciples of Jesus in the garden of Gethsemane after the arrest of their master. According to Mark and Matthew (Luke is silent on the incident), all the apostles abandoned Jesus and ran away (Mk 14:27–8; Mt 26:31–2). This shocking incident is explained away in both Gospels by a citation of the prophet Zechariah 13:7, 'I will strike the shepherd and the sheep will be scattered.' The justification of the apostles' desertion of Jesus by the necessity of the fulfilment of Scripture looks like an editorial manoeuvre, however, for, contrary to the evangelists' habit, no mention of the realization of prophecy is made when the escape of the disciples is reported. John, on the other hand, attributes to the intervention of Jesus the granting of free passage to the disciples by the soldiers. This smacks of typical Christian apologetics.

3. The real crux in the Passion story centres on the venue and nature of the night proceedings against Jesus and the identity of the priestly leader conducting them. In John, Jesus was taken to, and interrogated by, Annas, who then sent him to Caiaphas, and Caiaphas in turn delivered him to Pilate. In the Synoptics, Jesus is tried by the Sanhedrin under the presidency of Caiaphas.

Annas (Hanan) or Ananus son of Sethi was the most influential high priest in the first century AD. Appointed in AD 6 by Quirinius, governor of Syria, he held his job until a newly arrived Roman prefect of Judaea, Valerius Gratus, removed him from office in AD 15. The same Annas is also not only associated with the case of Jesus, but is mentioned again together with Caiaphas at the later inquiry into the apostles Peter and John by the Sanhedrin in Jerusalem (Acts 4:6). Annas' powerful influence with the Romans resulted in the elevation to the pontifical office not only of his son-in-law Caiaphas, but also, one after another, of five of his sons and one grandson.

There is nothing extraordinary in Jesus' appearance before Annas as we know from Josephus that former high priests often continued to play an important role in Jewish life in the first century AD. Indeed, if the case of Jesus was thought to be a complicated or delicate one, Annas was the obvious official to deal with it. His report to Caiaphas must have been that the easiest way of getting rid of Jesus was to hand over to Pilate this would-be Messiah as someone who claimed to be the King of the Jews, dirty words in Roman ears.

It is of primary importance to stress that in the Fourth Gospel *there is no Jewish trial*, there are no witnesses, and no sentence is pronounced by Jewish judges on religious or any other grounds. The only tribunal before which Jesus appeared in John was that of the Roman governor of Judaea. That the arrest and the questioning took place the day *before* Passover are also positively confirmed in John's account of the indictment of Jesus before Pontius Pilate. The versions of John and the Synoptics flatly contradict one another.

The Synoptic version of the trial of Jesus occurring at Passover night (or in the morning of Passover according to Luke) seems to be intrinsically vitiated. Both the timing of the hearing and the charge of blasphemy create apparently insoluble legal difficulties. According to the Mishnah, no capital sentence could be pronounced by the Sanhedrin on the day of the court hearing itself; it had to wait until the following day, allowing the judges to reflect on their verdict during the night. 'Therefore trials involving death penalty may not be held *on the eve of sabbath or on the eve of a feast day*' (Mishnah Sanhedrin 4:1; Betzah 5:2). That a court should not do business on a Sabbath is obvious. Apart from all other considerations, since the proceedings had to be recorded by two court clerks, the Mishnah's prohibition to write as few as two letters on the Sabbath (Shabbat 7:2) would exclude the recording of minutes and thereby render court proceedings impossible.

But many New Testament scholars object to the use of the Mishnah as a term of comparison for the study of the Gospels because of its date of redaction (*c.* AD 200). Be this as it may, the Mishnah passage is not the only relevant evidence. First-century AD sources, such as Philo and the Dead Sea Scrolls, also testify to the illegality of court business on Sabbaths/feast days. Thus Philo writes: 'Let us not ... abrogate the laws laid down for its [the Sabbath's] observance and ... institute [on that day] proceedings in court' (*Migration of Abraham* 91), and the Damascus Document from Qumran states just as firmly that 'no one shall judge' on the Sabbath day (10:17–18).

Caiaphas' attempt, reported in the Synoptics, to induce Jesus to incriminate himself would also have been illegal if the relevant rabbinic law decreeing invalid the admission of guilt by the accused without confirmation by witnesses was in force in the age of Jesus.

As for the crime of blasphemy with which Jesus was charged, its definition must next be examined. In the language of the Bible, in Philo and Josephus, as well as in secular Greek and in the Septuagint, the meaning of the concept of blasphemy lacks precision. In the Old Testament one can blaspheme the deity, but one can also blaspheme the king (Ex 22:28). Similarly in Josephus (and in the Acts of the Apostles) the verb is successively used with reference to disparaging God, the Jews, the ancestral laws of the Jews and their Law-giver Moses (*Against Apion* 1:143, 223, 279; Acts 6:11). Blasphemy, in other words, signifies any kind of disrespectful speech, but clearly not every disrespectful speech is punishable by death.

It may be argued that in the age of Jesus the attribution to a man of actions which are normally associated with God could also be considered blasphemous. For example, some Galilean scribes wondered whether Jesus was blaspheming when he promised forgiveness of sins to a paralysed man in Capernaum (Mk 2:7), yet none of them clamoured for Jesus' life. Indeed, in the terminology of charismatics healing and exorcism were the equivalent of forgiveness of sin, but since such charismatic acts were believed to be performed with the help of God, they did not entail anything religiously improper.

To establish the precise meaning of blasphemy, we must recall that from biblical times onwards the *legal language* used by Jews saw a special link between blasphemy and the divine *name* (Lev 24:11–16). Originally the prohibition concerned any irreverent speech about God, but by the start of the first century AD blasphemy came to be specifically linked to the pronunciation of the Tetragram. The four-lettered divine name, YHWH, was unutterable and had to be replaced even in prayer by substitutes such as Lord, Heaven or Temple. The protection of the name of the God of Israel went so far that both Philo (*Special Laws* 1:53) and Josephus (*Jewish Antiquities* 4:207; *Against Apion* 2:279) condemn abusive references to pagan deities lest Gentiles are impelled to retaliate and blaspheme the God of the Jews.

The Community Rule of Qumran seems to point in the

same direction when it strictly prohibits the enunciation of the sacrosanct divine Name in any circumstance. 'If any man has uttered the [Most] Venerable Name even frivolously, or as a result of shock or any other reason whatever, when reading the Book [the Bible] or blessing [reciting a prayer], he shall be dismissed, and shall return to the Council of the community no more' (6:27–7:2). The punishment at Qumran was irrevocable excommunication, the spiritual equivalent among the Essenes of the death penalty (Josephus, *Jewish War* 2:144).

Rabbinic literature lays down that the utterance of the sacrosanct Tetragram was an absolute requisite for someone to be charged with blasphemy: 'The blasphemer is not guilty unless he pronounces the Name' (Mishnah Sanhedrin 7:5). Reviling a substitute name was disapproved of, but did not carry the death penalty. It is apposite therefore to underline that in all three Synoptic Gospels Jesus is presented as employing a substitute name for God in his answer to the high priest and speaks not of the right hand of God, but of 'the right hand of the *Power*' (Mk 14:62; Mt 26:64; Lk 22:69). The alleged judgement of the Sanhedrin, 'You have heard his blasphemy' (Mk 14:64) appears therefore precipitate.

To recapitulate, no Jewish law of any age suggests that messianic claim amounted to the crime of blasphemy. Josephus refers to many an individual who prior to the outbreak of the first rebellion against Rome pretended to be the Messiah, and in the early second century AD Simeon Bar Kokhba was spoken of in the same terms, but none of them was accused of, or tried for, blasphemy.

It would therefore seem that the Synoptic tale of the night proceedings against Jesus lacks real foundation. To what, then, does it owe its existence? One may ask whether

Jesus' Jewish religious trial was built by Mark and his followers on a linguistic anachronism. The Synoptics take the Semitic metaphor 'Son of God', designating in the age of Jesus someone especially favoured by heaven (for instance, the royal Messiah), as the equivalent of their theological notion in the final decades of the first century AD, when it had already become among the Gentile Christians addressed by the Gospels the title of a person believed to share the nature of God in some way. In brief, Mark, Matthew and Luke appear to ascribe to Caiaphas their own understanding of Messiah=Son of God. As Rudolf Bultmann pertinently remarked, 'For the later Christian tradition Jesus' messianic claim, which was the chief issue between the Church and Judaism, could very well appear to be the ground of his condemnation' (*History of the Synoptic Tradition*, 1963, p. 270).

To put the matter into proper perspective, it is worth reflecting on a famous saying of Rabbi Abbahu, a third-century AD teacher from Caesarea, which is without any doubt a veiled criticism of Jesus. But observe the difference of attitude revealed in his words.

'If a man says to you, "I am God", he lies. "I am the Son of man" [a human being], he will be sorry at the end [as he will die]. "I will go up to heaven", he says so, but will not fulfil it' (Jerusalem Talmud Taanit 65b).

4. Another important issue is raised only in John, although it would have been useful for the Synoptics: Did Jewish courts have capital jurisdiction in the age of Jesus? In John Pilate suggests that Jesus should be dealt with by the chief priests' tribunal, but is reminded by them that the Sanhedrin had no power to order the execution of a Jewish criminal convicted by Jewish law: 'It is not lawful for us to put any man to death' (Jn 18:31).

Already in Christian antiquity some perspicacious Church fathers, wrestling with exegetical issues, interpreted the saying as alluding to the feast of Passover during which no execution could lawfully take place. 'They were not allowed to put any man to death because of the sanctity of the feast day,' writes St Augustine (*On the Gospel of John*, Tractate 114:4). St John Chrysostom makes a similar remark (*Homily on John* 83:4), echoing the Mishnah's prohibition of trying a capital case on the eve of Sabbath or of a festival (see p. 100).

In Old Testament times, during the existence of the independent Jewish kingdoms, biblical law did not distinguish between religious and civil issues, and secular and priestly judges dealt jointly with the administration of justice. The same combined legal authority functioned also under the Maccabaean-Hasmonaean high-priestly rulers (140–40BC). The most notorious affair was the summoning of the young Herod, governor of Galilee, before the supreme court in Jerusalem, made up of priests and lay Pharisees, under the presidency of the high priest Hyrcanus II. Herod was accused of putting a group of Jewish rebels to death without the due process of the law, but with Roman help and the complicity of Hyrcanus he escaped punishment (Josephus, *Jewish Antiquities*, 14:168–79).

A new situation arose with the establishment of direct Roman government in Judaea after the deposition of Herod's son Archelaus in AD 6 when the first Roman governor arrived with the power to convict and execute criminals (see p. 16). But did the granting of capital jurisdiction to the chief representative of Rome automatically abolish that of the Jewish high court in regard to offenders against the Mosaic Law? A number of New Testament scholars – by no means all of them dyed-in-the-wool fundamentalists – maintain with John that in the first century AD the Sanhedrin was forbidden to carry out executions. According to them, the order had to be issued by the Roman prefect or procurator. In support of this view there is a relatively late and somewhat vague talmudic statement implying that forty years before the destruction of the Temple the Sanhedrin lost its right to try capital cases (Jerusalem Talmud Sanhedrin 18a). However, apart from John, no historical source records such a change, datable to about AD 30. Should one none the less adopt the view of the Sanhedrin's incapacity to execute convicted criminals, the need to hand Jesus over to Pilate – on a new political charge – after his condemnation for blasphemy would become intelligible. But oddly, the Synoptics remain silent on the matter.

However, the opposite opinion, namely that the Sanhedrin continued to possess capital jurisdiction, can also marshal strong arguments. In the first place, common sense dictates that Roman governors would not interfere in religious or social matters lacking political dimension. For instance, adultery and rape carried the death penalty in Jewish law. Is it conceivable that each case had to be presented to the prefect? Above all, would any representative of Rome involve himself in purely religious matters such as blasphemy or idolatry?

Common sense is backed by literary and epigraphic evidence from the first century AD. It indicates that Jews were entitled to put to death both Jews and foreigners, even Roman citizens, if they caught them in the forbidden area of the Temple of Jerusalem. Philo of Alexandria explains that any Jewish intruder, even a priest, faced '*death without appeal*' if found in the innermost Holy of Holies of the sanctuary. Only the high priest could enter once a year, on the Day of Atonement. Philo further adds that the same prohibition applied not only to Jews, but also to 'other races' (*Embassy to Gaius* 212, 306–7). Josephus, in turn, explicitly mentions a warning engraved on slabs in Greek and Latin and displayed at regular intervals along the Temple boundaries, forbidding foreigners to cross the line on pain of death (*Jewish War* 5:194; *Jewish Antiquities* 15:417). An inscription found in Jerusalem and published by Charles Clermont-Ganneau in 1872 confirms Josephus. It reads: 'No foreigner is to enter within the balustrade and the embankment around the sanctuary. Whoever is caught will have *himself to blame for his ensuing death*.' The need for Roman approval before execution is nowhere mentioned in these sources. What is more, Josephus reports that Titus, the general of the besieging Roman forces and future emperor, reminded the Jews fighting in the Temple of the warnings in question and commented, 'And did we not permit you to put to death any who passed [the boundary wall], even were he Roman?' (*Jewish Antiquities* 6:125–6).

Actual examples point in the direction of the competence of the Sanhedrin to deal with capital cases. Even if we were to discount the stoning of the proto-martyr Stephen as possibly an act of mob violence rather than the execution of a judicial sentence, we still have to reflect on the two-year-long dispute (AD 58–60) between the Sanhedrin and the Roman procurators as to whether Jews or Romans should try Paul. It is clear from this that the members of the council, headed by the high priests Ananias son of Nedebaeus and Ishmael son of Phiabi, considered themselves competent to deal on their own with Paul, arrested in the Temple on the apparently erroneous charge of complicity in bringing a Gentile, the Ephesian Trophimus, into the prohibited area (Acts 21:29), which they considered as a capital crime (Acts: 23–5). Likewise, when in AD 62 the high priest Ananus son of Ananus arraigned James the brother of Jesus before the supreme council and sent him to his death by stoning, he was taken to task by the Roman governor Albinus, not for pronouncing and executing a capital sentence, but for convening a meeting of the Sanhedrin during the vacancy of the procuratorial office. He was accused of an administrative offence and not of the criminal charge of murder.

A further indirect confirmation of the Jewish high court's capital jurisdiction exercised even after the fall of Jerusalem in AD 70 comes from the early third century AD. The great Alexandrian Bible expert Origen, who lived in Caesarea between *c.* AD 230 and 250, in his letter to a learned Christian, Julius Africanus, describes the *Nasi* or chief rabbi as an official exercising with the emperor's consent as much power among the Jews as did the kings of the other nations. Origen continues: 'Trials are held secretly according to the Law and *some are condemned to death.* This is done neither in complete openness, nor without the knowledge of the [Roman] ruler' (Letter to Julius Africanus 20 [14]).

The hint at the quasi-secret character of the proceedings in capital cases may open a new perspective on the introduction of strangling as a non-biblical form of execution after the cessation of the Sanhedrin as a state institution in AD 70. The most common forms of execution, stoning and burning, had to be performed in the open in full public view. Strangling could be done quietly indoors.

In fact, it is most likely that during the procuratorial period the Roman and the Jewish legal systems were again and again in competition with each other. The authority which was the quickest to act tried and, when appropriate, executed the culprit. So, all things considered, one can make out a good case either for or against the Jewish high court's ability to try, sentence and execute Jesus. But if the view that the Sanhedrin had the power to impose and carry out the death sentence prevails, the fact that it referred the case of Jesus to Pilate would mean that it *chose* not to exercise its prerogative.

5. A less significant difference between John and the Synoptics relates to the presence of the mother of Jesus and 'the disciple whom he loved' at the foot of the cross. This is perfectly in line with the Fourth Gospel's devout attitude towards Mary, and is in sharp contrast with the Synoptics' outlook in which after their clash with Jesus in Galilee the family completely disappears from sight until and including the Passion (Mk 3:31–5; Mt 12:46–50; Lk 8:19–21).

6. A further difference between John and the Synoptics centres on Nicodemus' association with Joseph of Arimathea in the burial of Jesus. The mention in John's account of Nicodemus bringing with him a large quantity of spices pre-empts the need stated in the Synoptics for the Galilean women friends of Jesus to visit the tomb, after the Sabbath rest, on (Easter) Sunday morning to complete the unfinished burial rites (Mk 16:1; Mt 28:1; Lk 23:55–24:1).

7. Finally, some minor points on which John and the Synoptics differ relate to the sudden darkness that fell on Jerusalem during the last three hours of the life of Jesus (Mk 15:33; Mt 27:45; Lk 23:44). It is not presented as the realization of prophecy, but it is part of the Jewish eschatological imagery of the day of the Lord. It is to be treated as a literary rather than historical phenomenon notwithstanding naive scientists and over-eager television docu-

mentary makers, tempted to interpret the account as a datable eclipse of the sun. They would be barking up the wrong tree. The rending of the curtain of the Temple from top to bottom is another apocalyptic-eschatological symbol. Rabbinic literature lists various odd happenings forty years before the destruction of the Temple and speaks of Titus cutting the curtain of the sanctuary into two (Babylonian Talmud Gittin 56b). If, as is generally thought, the recording of the Synoptic Gospels took place after the fall of Jerusalem, these Jewish folk tales surrounding the great catastrophe of AD 70 may have cast their shadow on the evangelists' portrayal of the death of Jesus.

## 3. Comments on some peculiarities in Luke

Special material preserved in Luke alone and some of Luke's distinctive adjustments of Mark's narrative call for further exploration. The only additional story of historical relevance in Luke is the examination of Jesus by the ruler of Galilee, Herod Antipas (Lk 23:6–12). In its favour one can cite diplomatic courtesy, which is in fact a convenient attempt to 'pass the buck' first from Pilate to Herod and then from Herod back to Pilate. A similar, though one-sided, ploy between the Jewish authorities and the Roman governor is reported by Josephus in connection with Jesus son of Ananias, the charismatic who was making a nuisance of himself in Jerusalem during the feast of Tabernacles in AD 62 (*Jewish War* 6: 300–309). The Temple leaders, unable to silence the turbulent prophet by means of corporal punishment and a little worried by the possibility that this Jesus was a spokesman of God, handed him over to the Roman procurator Albinus to sort out the matter. He did, and after administering a severe beating to Jesus son of Ananias, he let him go.

Against the historicity of the Herod episode speaks the silence of the other three evangelists, and the fact that a visit to Antipas entailing a lengthy questioning by him and no doubt equally lengthy accusations by the chief priests are difficult to fit into the tight timetable of the Synoptics who place the crucifixion at nine o'clock in the morning. John's scenario with the crucifixion at noon could better accommodate the Herod excursus, but John knows nothing of it.

A number of other small variations also appear in Luke. Whilst in Mark and Matthew both crucified 'brigands' scoff at Jesus, Luke turns one of them into a decent human being who rebukes his fellow and begs for Jesus' help. Again Jesus' disturbing last cry, 'My God, my God, why hast thou forsaken me?' (Mark, Matthew) is replaced in Luke by the pious 'Father, into thy hands I commit my spirit.' At an earlier stage, Luke not only stops one of the sword-waving apostles in the garden of Gethsemane, but also miraculously heals the injured servant of the high priest. Finally, the harsh account of Mark that the only sympathizers watching the dying Jesus from a distance were a few women is replaced in Luke by the presence of all Jesus' acquaintances in addition to the women who had followed him from Galilee (Mk 15:40; Mt 27:55; Lk 23:49). Whether these extras correspond to reality or rather reflect Luke's compassionate temperament remains to be decided.

By now the full evidence has been laid out before the reader and all the arguments, pro and con, have been stated. All that remains is to propose a reconstruction of the real story of the Passion of Jesus and sketch the portraits of the protagonists of the drama.

# IV

## *The dénouement*

Readers expecting a dramatic unravelling of the plot as is customary in detective novels will be disappointed. Historical reality seems to be less unpredictable than fiction. In fact, most of the clues concealed in the Passion story have been fully or partially disclosed in the course of our earlier examination of the evidence. All we need to do now is to state the findings.

The most significant dilemma, which arises from the conflicting chronologies, is relatively easy to solve. The timing of the events in the Synoptic Gospels is quasi impossible. The sequence proposed by Mark and Matthew, and in a slightly more confused and hesitant way by Luke, is hindered at every inch of the way. It is hard to imagine in a Jewish setting of the first century AD that a capital case would be tried at night, and in particular on the feast of Passover. It is equally unlikely that the leaders of the Jewish religion, neglecting their Temple duties, would act as accusers in a hearing held by the Roman governor on the morning of the fifteenth day of Nisan and spend the rest of Passover in following Jesus to Golgotha and watching him die on the cross. I omit rehearsing the embarrassing and ill-conceived scenario of a Jewish religious trial in which the testimony of all the witnesses is thrown out, yet the accused is condemned to death on more than dubious grounds as a blasphemer and afterwards subjected to abuse by the judges themselves. Without explaining why, these same judges then manufacture a new charge and agree to transfer the case to a different jurisdiction.

The scheme presented by John avoids all these pitfalls. If Jesus is taken into custody during the evening of the fourteenth day of Nisan and tried by Pilate in the early morning of the eve of Passover, a hurried appearance of the chief priests before the governor and their disappearance after sentencing can be envisaged without difficulty. In conformity with their obligations towards their Roman masters, they act as prosecutors against a suspected Jewish revolutionary who, in their judgement, is a threat to the peace and well-being of the community. They have done their duty; their conscience is clear; let the Romans do the dirty work. In John there is no illegal night trial, indeed there is no Jewish religious trial at all: Jesus is only interrogated by the most experienced and wiliest of judges, the former high priest Annas. The main problem one has to face if John's version is preferred comes from the late date of the Fourth Gospel (*c.* 100–110); as a rule the Synoptics represent the more primitive version of the Jesus story. Nevertheless, the generally greater historical reliability of Mark does not necessarily exclude the possibility of John occasionally inheriting a more authentic tradition. In the case of the chronology of the Passion John is clearly independent of the Synoptics. His timing makes sense; that of the Synoptics does not.

The Johannine version of the trial of Jesus is partially supported by Luke, who like the author of the Fourth Gospel has no knowledge of a night session of the Sanhedrin. His transposition of a garbled compact version of the alleged night proceedings to the morning meeting of the court is attributable to his desire to stay as close as possible to his model, Mark.

Did Roman soldiers participate in the arrest of Jesus as John may insinuate? All things considered, I doubt it. There is no clue anywhere in the Gospels hinting at Roman suspicion in regard to Jesus. Also, the military notions used are inappropriate. A cohort comprising 600 men was too large a force, and a tribune too senior an officer, for the job. The Temple police led by Jews sufficed. They were able to implement the orders of the chief priests, official guardians of peace, during the dangerous pilgrimage period when Pilate himself came to Jerusalem and was keeping an eye on them.

The trial of Jesus before Pilate, once we disregard the evangelists' determination to exculpate the governor, raises no real problems, and the death sentence after an indictment for sedition is exactly what one would expect. The only uncertainty concerns the Passover amnesty. The four evangelists unanimously attest it; Roman sources, Josephus, Philo and the rabbis are equally unanimously silent on the matter. Barabbas, the lucky winner, is a totally unknown entity. According to the normal rules of historical research one should query both the custom of amnesty and the existence of Barabbas. Yet the episode has all the appearances of being real. It is not important enough for the main story to need to be invented. Nothing essential hinges on it. No doubt the Jews' choice of Barabbas rather than Jesus makes them look extremely prejudiced, but they are portrayed in the darkest colours even without that choice. The fact that the incident has no specific purpose is in its favour. Moreover, public knowledge of the forthcoming amnesty would account for the presence of a crowd at the praetorium. Supposing the people present were mostly supporters of Barabbas and that popular clamour influenced Pilate's decision about whom he would pardon, Jesus, deserted by his Galilean followers, was bound to be the loser. Hence I hesitantly cast my vote for the authenticity of the Barabbas episode.

Of the repeated scenes of insult, violence and mockery the one involving the Roman soldiers, between the flogging and the crucifixion, appears to be the most likely (see Josephus, *Jewish War* 5:449).

Again, the absence of purpose for inventing it is the strongest argument in favour of the historicity of the Simon of Cyrene episode.

Among the three verbalized final cries of Jesus, *Eloi, Eloi, lama sabachthani?* – My God, my God, why hast thou forsaken me? (Mark, Matthew); 'Father, into thy hands I commit my spirit' (Luke); and 'It is finished' (John), the last two are theologically correct and reassuring formulations, whereas the first, preserved in Aramaic, is unexpected, disquieting and in consequence more probable. It is noteworthy that this is the only prayer of Jesus in which God is not addressed as Father.

As for the identity of the sympathizers who followed Jesus to the cross, Mark's version of some women including Mary Magdalene, another Mary and Salome proves best how abandoned Jesus was in his hour of need. Matthew speaks of *many* women in addition to the three named ones, and Luke brings along all Jesus' acquaintances (male and female?) as well as the Galilean women. John cuts down the number of attendants but raises their standing. They comprise the mother of Jesus, his maternal aunt and Mary Magdalene as well as his beloved disciple. The clear impression one gathers is that Luke, Matthew and John deliberately try to smooth the picture. Mark's terseness is preferable.

This leaves us with the final dilemma: was Jesus buried by Joseph of Arimathea alone (Synoptics) or by Joseph and Nicodemus (John)? As there are no special arguments in favour of either, the question may be left unanswered. Indeed, both alternatives are organically integrated into the story. The hasty burial of the body by Joseph explains the need for a completion of the funeral rites in the Synoptics with the subsequent visit of three women to the tomb after the end of the Sabbath. In John, on the other hand, Nicodemus brings spices, so that nothing remains undone regarding the ritual, and if Mary Magdalene returns to the grave, it is out of piety rather than to attend to unfinished business.

In the Prologue I have asked the question: What really did happen on the day of the crucifixion of Jesus nearly 2,000 years ago?

Here now is the answer.

1. On Thursday evening, when the *eve* of Passover (14 Nisan) began, Jesus held a common meal with his apostles which turned out to be his last. It was not a Passover supper, nor did it contain the institution of the Eucharist.

2. He was arrested by an armed unit of the Jewish Temple police sent by the chief priests and led by Judas.

3. He was taken to the former high priest Annas for interrogation and sent by him to the house of the high priest Caiaphas where he was kept during the night.

4. On Friday morning (14 Nisan) the Sanhedrin held a consultation and decided to arraign Jesus before the tribunal of the Roman governor and charge him with sedition.

5. Pilate heard the charges of sedition arising from Jesus' alleged (political) claim that he was the King of the Jews,

but proposed to handle the case in the framework of the supposedly customary Passover amnesty. The assembled Jewish crowd hoping to obtain the release of another prisoner voted for Barabbas who was subsequently set free.

6. Jesus was condemned to crucifixion by Pilate and his priestly accusers left the scene.

7. As a preliminary to his crucifixion, Jesus was scourged. He was also subjected to mockery and beating by the Roman soldiers.

8. Simon of Cyrene was forced to help Jesus to carry the cross to Golgotha.

9. Jesus was crucified at noon on the eve of Passover (14 Nisan).

10. He was heard crying in Aramaic, '*Eloi, Eloi lama sabachthani?*' and died at 3 p.m. on the same day, watched by a small group of Galilean women. Neither his apostles nor his family attended.

11. With Pilate's permission Joseph of Arimathea, or Joseph and Nicodemus, laid the body of Jesus in a new rock tomb shortly before the onset of the feast of Passover and the Sabbath on Saturday, 15 Nisan.

Finally, on the basis of astronomical calculation it can be argued that in AD 30, the year of the Passion, Passover celebrated at the full moon on 15 Nisan fell on Saturday, 8 April, and that consequently Jesus, crucified on the eve of Passover (14 Nisan), died on Friday, 7 April AD 30.

Thus ends the story of the Passion. The Resurrection narratives open a new chapter in the biography of Jesus and cannot be discussed here.

# Epilogue
## The leading actors of the Passion story

So far the examination of the Passion accounts has been mostly analytical. It is advisable therefore to end it on a constructive note and sketch the protagonists of the drama, the Jewish people, Caiaphas, Pontius Pilate and Jesus himself in four vignettes. The evangelists, above all Matthew and John, paint a deeply antipathetic picture of the first two. They all put Pontius Pilate in the best possible light. As for Jesus, patently the central figure, he plays a subdued role, quite often even refusing to answer questions.

### The Jews

General Jewish hostility to Jesus is not manifest everywhere in the Gospel story. The Prologue has underlined the difference between the antipathy verging on viciousness encountered by Jesus in Jerusalem during the last day of his life and the warmth of the Galilean population towards the charismatic healer and teacher from Nazareth. His sympathetic reception in his home country was apparently also matched by a cordial acclaim given him on his entry into the holy city. But from the moment of his arrest not only all the Jewish leaders, but also the entire Jewish crowd, both at the palace of Pilate and on Golgotha, are said to have displayed a profound hatred towards him.

This negative unanimity is astounding as it contradicts the evidence expressed elsewhere in the New Testament. Prior to the arrest, the chief priests hesitated to make an immediate move against Jesus because they feared massive popular outrage. Later in the Acts of the Apostles the Jewish leaders of Jerusalem are not depicted as blindly inimical to the followers of Jesus. Peter attributed ignorance or lack of understanding rather than ill will to the chief priests (Acts 3:17). The famous Pharisee rabbi Gamaliel pleaded for fairness towards the apostles before the high court (Acts 5:34–9) and even during a stormy meeting of the Sanhedrin dealing with Paul, accused of preaching against the Law, the Pharisee members of the council openly supported him: 'We find nothing wrong with this man. What if a spirit or an angel spoke to him?' (Acts 23:9). The only rational explanation consists in assigning the hostile tendency of the Gospels to the increasingly powerful anti-Judaism of the early Gentile Church. In fact the Jews as such cannot be held guilty for their leaders' action resulting in the tragedy of Jesus.

## Caiaphas

Caiaphas, the high priest, and the chief priests are the villains of the Passion story. Does this portrait reflect historical reality or is it also the product of the theological and apologetic speculation of the evangelists? Their thoroughgoing antagonism to Jews seems to suggest that they had given up hope of any further successful mission among the Jews. Also, by the time of the redaction of the Passion narratives the synagogue and the Church had already split. Late first-century AD (Gentile) Christians perceived the Jews as *the* enemies. The 'they against us' situation prevailing by then could easily be retrojected to the time of the

Passion itself and lead to the de-Judaization of Jesus and his followers. Since Jesus was seen as persecuted by *the Jews*, he ceased to be apprehended as belonging to the Jewish people and was simply turned into a Christian.

To judge his real role in the Passion, Caiaphas' likely motivation needs to be investigated. It may be argued that if he saw, in his capacity of high priest, any potential political danger in Jesus, he would react out of fear of Roman criticism for failing to maintain order in Jerusalem combined with a sentiment of duty to protect the Jewish community against foreseeable Roman excesses. His ultimate purpose, summed up in the principle that the whole nation is more important than a single individual, was no doubt based on a misjudgement of Jesus, but it cannot be qualified as wholly dishonourable. Arguably he did what a man in his position had to do, and this could occasionally entail the unpalatable duty of sacrificing an individual for the common good. Besides, the fact that he managed to keep his job for eighteen years when most of his predecessors and successors were sacked in their first or second year in office proves that Joseph Caiaphas was a shrewd operator. He was not a satanic figure, however, just an efficient quisling, responsible for handing over Jesus to the Romans in full awareness of the likely outcome. Nevertheless, the ultimate *legal responsibility* for the crucifixion lies with Pilate and the Roman empire. In all probability it was a major miscarriage of justice as Jesus does not seem to have been motivated by political ambitions.

## Pilate

Pilate's portrait by the evangelists is that of a sensible if irresolute judge. He no doubt took with a pinch of salt the accusations levelled against Jesus by the chief priests, suspecting intra-Jewish jealousies, and Jesus' unco-operative behaviour baffled him. He was prepared to let him go – maybe after a good beating – or make him candidate for the Passover amnesty. Pilate's almost abject pleading with the priestly leaders and the Jewish crowd, and his fear of a riot seem to be baseless and out of character. An order to his legionaries would have made all the vociferous Jews run for their lives. On the whole, the Roman governor of the Gospels is pictured as a man who believed Jesus to be innocent but allowed himself to be manipulated by the Jews and ended by sending their king to the cross.

However, the Pilate of the New Testament has little in common with the Pilate of history. Indeed, Philo of Alexandria and Flavius Josephus, the two outstanding Jewish writers of that age, have a great deal to report about the prefect of Judaea, and what they have to say is far from flattering. Philo (*Embassy to Gaius* 299–305) quotes the opinion of the Jewish king Herod Agrippa I who, writing to the emperor Gaius Caligula, portrays Pilate as a stubborn, irascible, vindictive, naturally inflexible, self-willed and obdurate man who committed insults, robberies, outrages and wanton injuries. He also became notorious for venality and many acts of grievous cruelty as well as for numerous executions without trial.

The Pilate of Josephus is also a harsh, inconsiderate and ruthless official. Soon after his arrival in Judaea, he broke with the custom of his predecessors and tactlessly offended the religious sensibilities of the Jews of Jerusalem by commanding his soldiers to carry into the city Roman standards bearing the image of the emperor. He is known to have ordered the massacre of unarmed Jews who protested against his unlawful appropriation of the *Corban* (offering) from the Temple treasury. Among the calamities caused by Pilate, Josephus lists the crucifixion of Jesus. A further criminal act, a murderous attack on a group of Samaritans, finally forced Vitellius, Roman legate of Syria, to relieve Pilate of his governorship and send him to Rome to account to the emperor for his misdeeds ( *Jewish War* 2:169–77; *Jewish Antiquities* 18:35–89). These negative representations by first-century Jewish writers, who were by no means anti-Roman, find a surprising echo even in the New Testament. The Gospel of Luke once mentions a massacre of Galilean pilgrims 'whose blood Pilate had mixed with their sacrifices' (Lk 13:1).

The only argument that can be quoted in favour of the Gospel portrayal of Pilate is the apparent general unwillingness of Roman magistrates to touch Jewish matters with religious ramifications. It is sufficient to cite the refusal of Gallio, proconsul of Achaia, to adjudicate in the quarrel between Paul and the Jewish leaders of Corinth (Acts 18:14–15).

All told, the Pilate picture of the Passion story is best held to be fiction, devised by the evangelists with a view to currying favour with Rome, in whose empire the nascent Church was developing. Christianity being generally unpopular in Roman eyes – Tacitus calls it a 'pernicious superstition' (*Annals* 15:44) – it was in the interest of the Gospel writers to placate the authorities. Also, by the time of the recording of the Passion narratives the Jewish rebellion had been put down by the armies of Vespasian and Titus. It was therefore politically doubly correct to blame the Jews for the murder of Christ and to absolve the Roman Pontius Pilate. In some corners of the Christian world he was treated as a crypto-believer and ended up as a saint in the Coptic Church of Egypt. The spin doctors of antiquity were no less inventive than their modern successors.

## Jesus

The Passion accounts on their own are unsuitable for drawing a true picture of Jesus. In the course of his arrest in the Synoptics and in his answer to Annas in John Jesus pleaded innocence in politics: he had no secret agenda and always taught in public. The otherworldly superiority of the Johannine Christ figure mirrors the highly evolved theology of the Fourth Gospel, which was far in advance on the historical Jesus. The mighty soldiers fell to the ground when he told them that he was the man they were looking for, and Pilate, the representative of the greatest world power, was frightened by his mysterious silence.

Nevertheless, there are two incidents in the Passion which may convey a deep perception of the real Jesus. Even during his Last Supper, he is drawn by the Synoptics as hopeful and looking forward to completing his mission. He made a vow not to touch wine again until the coming of the kingdom of God (see p. 37). If he had been aware of his impending demise, such a vow of abstemiousness would have been empty of meaning. Finally, the Aramaic words *Eloi, Eloi lama sabachthani?* bear all the appearances of a genuine cry. Representing the consternation of a man of faith at the sudden realization that God would not come to his rescue, the exclamation is a piously inspired prayer of disbelief. But 'Why hast thou forsaken me?' is followed in Mark and Matthew by another loud clamour, the words of which, perhaps in order to enhance the dramatic effect, remain untold. Did they repeat the quintessential prayer of Jesus, 'Thy will be done'?

# Bibliography

Blinzler, Josef, *The Trial of Jesus* (Mercier Press, Cork, 1959).

Winter, Paul, *On the Trial of Jesus* (W. de Gruyter, Berlin, 1961, 2nd edn 1974).

Sherwin-White, A. N., *Roman Society and Roman Law in the New Testament* (Clarendon Press, Oxford, 1963).

Brandon, S. G. F., *The Trial of Jesus of Nazareth* (Batsford, London, 1968).

Catchpole, D. R., *The Trial of Jesus* (E. J. Brill, Leiden, 1971).

Cohn, H. H., *The Trial and Death of Jesus* (Weidenfeld & Nicolson, London, 1972).

Sloyan, G. S., *Jesus on Trial* (Fortress Press, Philadelphia, 1973).

Goodman, Martin, *The Ruling Class of Judea* (Cambridge University Press, Cambridge, 1987).

Millar, Fergus, 'Reflections on the Trials of Jesus', in *A Tribute to Geza Vermes* (JSOT Press, Sheffield, 1990, pp. 355–81).

Crossan, J. D., *The Historical Jesus* (HarperSanFrancisco, 1991).

Sanders, E. P., *The Historical Figure of Jesus* (Allen Lane, London, 1993).

Brown, R. E., *The Death of the Messiah*, vols. I-II (Doubleday, New York, 1994)

Fredriksen, Paula, *Jesus of Nazareth, the King of the Jews* (Knopf, New York, 1999).

Vermes, G., *The Authentic Gospel of Jesus* (Allen Lane, London, 2003).

Classical sources

Josephus, Flavius, *The Jewish War – The Jewish Antiquities – The Life – Against Apion*, in *Josephus with an English Translation*, vols. I–IX, by H. St J. Thackeray and L. H. Feldman, Loeb Classical Library, London/New York, 1926–65.

Philo of Alexandria, in *Philo with an English Translation*, vols. I–X by F. H. Colson and G. H. Whitaker, Loeb Classical Library, London/New York, 1962.

Tacitus, Cornelius, *Annals with an English Translation* by J. Jackson, Loeb Classical Library, London/New York, 1937.

# Index

### The Authentic Gospel of Jesus

Acclaimed religious scholar Geza Vermes subjects all the sayings of Jesus to brilliantly informed scrutiny. Profoundly aware of the limits of our knowledge but immersed in what we do have—both the "official" gospels and associated Jewish and early Christian texts—Vermes sifts through every quote ascribed to Jesus to let the reader get as close as possible to the charismatic Jewish healer and moralist who changed the world. The result is a book that creates a revolutionary and unexpected picture of Jesus.

"Wonderfully accessible . . . open minded. . . . This book will demand that Christians rethink their faith."          —*Sunday Times* (London)
*ISBN 0-14-100360-X*

### The Changing Faces of Jesus

This groundbreaking historical exploration asks "Who was the real Jesus?" How was a Palestinian charismatic leader transformed by later generations into the heavenly savior who is the focus of the Christian Church? Did Jesus' own teachings lead to his divine characterization? Or did the church-centered needs of gentile Christianity hide his true face, obscuring the religion he preached and practiced? With unique authority, sensitivity, and insight, renowned scholar Geza Vermes explores these complex questions by examining the New Testament writings and placing them in the context of contemporary Jewish civilization in the first century. Starting with the elevated, divine figure of Christ presented in the most recent Gospel, the Gospel of John, Vermes travels back through earlier accounts of Jesus' life to reveal the true historical figure.

"Masterly. . . . Those who want to understand the historical Jesus and the evolving ways in which he was perceived in the following decades can do no better than to read this book."
—E. P. Sanders, *The New York Review of Books*
*ISBN 0-14-219602-9*

### The Complete Dead Sea Scrolls in English

The discovery of the Dead Sea Scrolls in the Judean desert between 1947 and 1956 transformed our understanding of the Hebrew Bible, early Judaism, and the origins of Christianity. These extraordinary scrolls appear to have been hidden in the caves at Qumran by members of the Essene community, a Jewish sect existing before and during the time of Jesus.

Fifty years after the scrolls' first discovery, and following the release of the scroll texts to scholars in 1991, this revised and expanded edition of *The Dead Sea Scrolls in English* crowns a lifetime of research by the esteemed Qumran scholar Geza Vermes. This is the most complete and authoritative scrolls edition available: it contains superb translations of all the texts sufficiently well-preserved to be rendered into English.

The authority, clarity, and remarkable literary qualities of these translations are immediately evident. There are brief introductions to each document and at the beginning of each chapter detailed historical, cultural, and religious background is provided. *The Complete Dead Sea Scrolls in English* is essential reading for anyone interested in ancient Judaism and early Christianity. Here, for scholars, students, and the general reader, are the texts which endure as the non-biblical center of Judeo-Christianity and the foundations of Western literary traditions.

"An excellent collection of texts . . . Vermes' translations are the most accurate and the most readable, and . . . the most accessible."
—Lawrence H. Schiffman, *Los Angeles Times Book Review*

"An excellent up-to-date report on the Dead Sea Scrolls . . . will enable the general public to read the nonbiblical scrolls and to judge for themselves their importance."
—Joseph A. Fitzmyer, *The New York Times Book Review*

*ISBN 0-14-044952-3*